Rural Tourism in Darjeeling Himalayas

(A Case Study)

Dr. Ananya Guha Roy

ISBN 9798894754932

Contents

List of Tables

Preface

Nowadays, rural tourism has developed into a brand-new type of travel activity that helps society on an economic, cultural and social level. Rural tourism has been able to preserve values and beliefs, safeguard the environment, create employment opportunities, lessen unemployment, promote local handicrafts, increase stakeholder and local people's income and capital, encourage the production of organic food, and foster the development of infrastructure, as well as open up opportunities for sustainable and economic development in rural areas. The purpose of this study is to identify the motivating factors, advantages, potentials, obstacles, problems for future research and sustainable development of rural tourism as well as the effects of rural tourism on the villagers' quality of life. In this study, Takdah, Lamahatta, Chatakpur and Sittong these four rural tourist locations in the Darjeeling Hills are examined in terms of the facilities for tourist attractions, the behavioural and functional characteristics of visitors, and the difficulties faced by business owners. On the basis of questionnaires, 100 persons were questioned, mostly the owners and stakeholders. The method of random sampling was used to choose the owners and tourists. Both qualitative and quantitative approaches have been employed as data analysis methodologies. Maps have been created using Arc GIS. In terms of conclusions, the study gives a general review of rural tourism in two separate locations that promote sustainable, rural, and economic growth. Opportunities for employment are made available through rural tourism. It accelerates the expansion of the service industry. It could be a viable way to sustainably preserve rural ecosystems. It lessens the gap between rural and urban regions, putting the latter on the path to growth. Sustainable development will be ensured by environmental enhancements, landscape preservation, and resource conservation.

In the Darjeeling Hills, the research examines how rural tourism contributes to socioeconomic, cultural and environmental development that is ultimately sustainable. Rural tourism has the potential to conserve the environment, raise revenue, offer job opportunities, lower unemployment, and maintain cultural values and beliefs.

Seventy percent of the population of Darjeeling lives in remote rural regions with little or no connectivity infrastructure. Due to the exceedingly difficult access to the market, there is an exacerbated system of exploitation, and farmers receive relatively little compensation for their agricultural output. Promoting, enabling and building people's organizations is one of the most efficient methods to escape this shackle. One new activity that will result from these organisations' strengthening is rural or community-based tourism. The first hotel, The Darjeeling Family Hotel, wasn't built until 1938, when tourism was first introduced. Until 1975, the government did nothing to encourage or interfere with the private management of tourism. In order to provide tourists with fundamental knowledge about tourism attractions, the West Bengal Tourism Development Corporation and the Tourism Department of the West Bengal Government were established in November 1975 and 1978 respectively. The location that has been selected for the current study has been identified as a cultural region where the components of the landscape are intimately connected. The northern region of the Indian state of West Bengal is home to Darjeeling, sometimes referred to as the "queen of the Himalayas." The main objective of this study is to investigate the patterns and growth of tourism in the Darjeeling Hills and their effects on rural development for the rural poor's sustainable life. In this hilly region, tourism is a significant source of revenue and employment for the local inhabitants. Each year, travellers spend around 70 crores of rupees. Every year, Darjeeling welcomes 50,000 overseas visitors in addition to about 3.5 million domestic visitors. Everyone profits from tourism, from the chai vendor to the hotel owner. In addition to raising revenue and boosting demand for regional goods, tourism has a multiplier impact. This is referring to the process through which tourist spending ripples through the economy and sparks more economic activity. It further demonstrates that the rural population's economy, which is both directly and indirectly related to tourism, has significantly improved as a result of the growth of village tourism in the Darjeeling Hills.

Due to a shortage of suitable hotels and other forms of visitor lodging in Darjeeling Hills' rural regions, the idea of homestays has thrived, enhancing local living. The majority of Darjeeling residents still view tourism as a benefit, but few people have really questioned whether it truly is. We have observed negative effects on Darjeeling's ecosystem ever since it became the focus of tourist. During the tourist season, Darjeeling's resources are under a lot of stress. People in Darjeeling, which is renowned for its water issue, endure shortages of everything from fuel to water. Even if mass tourism does penetrate rural regions, the consequences it will have on cultural norms, value systems, and, as already noted, the environment and health need to be evaluated and examined in order to find a workable solution.

– Dr Ananya Guha Roy

Chapter - I

Introduction

I.1. Introduction:

Travelling and staying in locations outside of one's home surroundings for leisure and pleasure is known as tourism. It is the movement of people to locations outside of their immediate area for leisure and to pursue a variety of objectives. According to McIntosh and Goeldner (McIntosh and Goeldner, 1986, p. 1), tourism is "the sum of the phenomena and relationships arising from the interaction of tourists, business suppliers, host governments, and host communities in the process of attracting and hosting these tourists and other visitors". Rural tourism is a growing trend in the tourism industry that has evolved not only as a potential source of income but also as a mode of recreation for city people who want to escape the hectic pace of the city. Rural tourism is the practise of exploring livelihoods, various traditions, social norms, and religious beliefs in rural places while allowing the local population to advance their socioeconomic status. It is primarily nature-based. It falls under the development categories of "Rural Development" and "Sustainable Development." It takes various forms since it promotes cultural variety and broadens people's perspectives on life. It is one of the ways that rural communities strive to increase profitability and efficiency because it not only provides jobs for people but also nurtures various socio-cultural and intellectual values.

The present study has evaluated the value of rural tourism to the long-term viability of the region, it's socio-economic status, rural development and the significance of governmental policies and their effects on rural tourism.

I.2. Conceptual Framework:

I.2.1. Tourism:

According to an early lexicon, tourism is the philosophy and practice of visiting and travelling for pleasure. Hunziker and Kraft (1942)[1] defined tourism as the giving of tours and receiving of accommodations to strangers without establishing a permanent residence or engaging in any business that might generate income.

Based on the previous definitions, which state that tourism is the involvement of non-residents in travel, brief stays in the destination tours, and stays unconnected to an activity that generates income, A.K. Bhatia (1991)[2] defined the following components of tourism. A particular class of travelers who are unfamiliar with the places they visit hence find tourism to be a pleasant and leisure activity they enjoy. Tourism, according to Richardson and Fluker (2004)[3], is a temporary journey that

---

1   *Hunziker, W., Kraft, K. (1942). "General Tourist Theory". The Outline of General Tourism Science, Vol. 26, No. 3.*

2   *Bhatia, A. K. (1991). Tourism Development: Principles and Practices. Sterling Publishers Private Limited, New Delhi.*

3   *Richardson, J. I. and Fluker, M. (2004); 'Understanding and Managing Tourism'. Frenchs Forest, NSW: Pearson Education Australia.*

take people from one place to another after leaving their home base with the goal of unwinding, enjoying leisure time, and satisfying a variety of desires rather than trying to make a living in the popular locations.

1.2.2.   Rural Tourism:

The Romanticism movement in the late eighteenth century is where rural tourism first emerged. As a response to industrialism, Romanticism first emerged in the ordinary world. Current rural tourism started after World War II, but the first unique visits in a while were based on the event concept (Lane, 2009)[4].

With the growth of the global economy came the emergence of rural tourism, which provides a range of benefits including the improvement of rural life, the preservation of rural culture and heritage, the development of infrastructure, and the creation of jobs. All facets of development like social, economic, and cultural are benefitted from rural tourism. Additionally, it promotes environmental growth. Not only does it aid in the development of rural areas, but it also benefits the surrounding communities and the local populace. It benefits the rural area's

---

4   Lane, B. (2009). "Rural Tourism: An Overview", The SAGE Handbook of Tourism Studies, (Ed. Tazim Jamal and Mike Robinson), SAGE Publications, Vol.1, No. 1.

development as well as the adjacent communities and the inhabitants that live there. Travel to isolated rural areas has been made easier by technical improvements like the worldwide internet, telephone services, and credit card use over cell phone networks as well as the infrastructure facilities for rural tourism including transportation, vehicle trends, and auto ownership. One of the most effective modern strategies for rural growth and development is rural tourism (Dashper, 2014)[5].

However, rural tourism offers a potential solution to some of the issues including a shrinking population and the loss of individual job opportunities that precede the rapid decline of agriculture. As a means of bringing more money into rural regions, encouraging growth and job creation, and starting to reverse the rural decline, several states and regional governments have embraced rural tourism. Rural tourism is viewed as a strategy to strengthen rural economies, provide employment, and halt the decline of rural areas. Rural attractions and activities, infrastructure, accessibility, various marketing corporations, and data models are all part of rural tourism (Irshad, 2010)[6]. Typically, rural tourism generates enough revenue to support itself (Frederick, 1992)[7].

I.2.3.   **Rural Tourism in the Global Context:**

Beginning in the early 1970s, rural tourism has been more well-liked all around the world. But the idea didn't really take off until the late eighteenth century, when it really took off (Lane, 2009). Rural tourism undoubtedly started in Western Europe before slowly spreading to North America, Australia, New Zealand, Asia (Japan), and Eastern Europe (Lane, 2009)[8]. The history of North American rural tourism

---

5   *Dashper, K. (2014); 'Rural Tourism: An International Perspective', Cambridge Scholars Publishing, Newcastle, UK.*

6   *Irshad, H. (2010); 'Rural Tourism - An Overview, Agriculture and Rural Development', Government of Alberta, Rural Development Division, October 2010.*

7   *Frederick, M. (1992); 'Tourism as a Rural Economic Development Tool: An Exploration of the Literature', U.S. Department of Agriculture, Economic Research Service*

8   *Ibid.*

development highlights the United States' experience in Canada. The growth of tourism in the countryside is a result of unplanned tourism as well as American economic and financial realities. Local qualities were used as the main basis to draw tourists and enhance marketing strategies. As a technique for boosting the economy in rural areas of the United States, rural tourism has gained importance (Gartner, 2004)[9]. The Alberta government defines rural tourism as a national experience that encompasses a wide range of attractions and activities that happen outside of major cities (Irshad, 2010)[10]. All of the European Union's member states use rural tourism as a significant tool for economic growth, which is supported by the industry's financial, social, ecological, and spatial potential. According to Kutay and Mashid (2016), distinctive biological landscapes, the agrarian economy, and traditional innovation greatly contribute to rural tourism and are crucial to rural development. Due to its geographical characteristics, diversified landscapes ideal for various forms of amusement, enjoyment of food, historical narratives, vibrant social legacy, etc., Serbia offers good conditions for rural tourist management in Eastern Europe. In addition to improving the resiliency and revitalization of rural life, this type of tourism could make a significant contribution to environmental protection. The Republic of Serbia possesses enormous common skills, but they are not being developed to the highest standards or shared with the public, which prevents them from being fully utilized (Dordevic, Susic, and Janjic, 2019)[11].

In Asia, rural tourism is a valuable industry that has numerous financial, ecological, sociocultural, and environmental advantages. Rural tourism in Nepal is still in its infancy, but it faces a number of difficulties with regard to administration and viability. Rural tourism is becoming more prevalent outside of such areas due to the growing environmental

---

9   *Gartner, W.C (2004); 'Rural Tourism Development in USA'; International Journal of Tourism Research, Vol.6 (3), May-June*

10   *Ibid.*

11   *Dordevic, Z. D., Susic, V., Janjic, I. (2019). "Perspectives of Development of Rural Tourism of the Republic Of Serbia", Economic Themes, Vol.1 No.1.*

issues in urban areas, particularly Kathmandu and other significant cities (Upadhyay, 2016)[12].

In small developing nations like Bhutan, rural tourism is regarded as a viable and efficient method of achieving gross national happiness. With well defined policies and objectives, the Bhutanese government has worked hard to develop rural tourism and earn income from it. The availability of rural tourism goods in Bhutan has increased demand from both national and foreign tourists (Dorji and Kinley, 2017)[13].

1.3.   Types of Rural Tourism:

As contrast to a mass visitor, rural tourism is usually referred to as alternative tourism. It is a form of tourist expansion that benefits various socioeconomic communities while utilizing resources in rural areas. It is divided into four categories based on its various attributes as follows:

i) **Nature Tourism**: Environmentally responsible recreation is the main aim of nature tourism. It is a type of ecotourism meant to improve both the local populace's quality of life and environmental protection. It is based on natural attractions including the surrounding area's scenic splendor, trekking, hiking, camping in the woods, bird-watching, and forest safaris, among others. It promotes the conservation of natural resources and the improvement of the value of the natural areas. As nature tourism plays a bigger role in the local economy, communities are more motivated to preserve their last remaining natural areas for animal lovers. The tourism

---

12   *Upadhyay, P. (2016). "Envisaged for Sustainable Rural Development: Viability and Challenges of Rural Tourism in Nepal", Repositioning, Vol. 1, No. 1.*

13   *Dorji P., Kinley (2017). "Rural Tourism in Bhutan: A Tool to Achieve Gross National Happiness", Journal of Hospitality Tourism, Vol. 4, No. 2, March.*

industry has always relied heavily on nature tourism (Spychala and Sylwia, 2013)[14].

ii) **Cultural Tourism:** It focuses on the way of life and culture of the locals. By presenting the community's extensive cultural heritage, it encourages both culture and tourism. Because it concentrates around a number of cultural events hosted by various ethnic groups, it is seasonal. It alludes to the growth of tourism in a variety of contexts, including those involving aesthetics, inspiration, historic preservation, and so on (Richards, 2018). Cultural tourism refers to the expression of cultural indicators such as folklore, ancient heritage, various arts, and so forth in tourist sites. (Mousavi et al, 2016).[15]

iii) **Health Tourism:** Health tourism is a well-known subset of rural tourism that emphasizes health and athletic pursuits while focusing on affluence and eminence pharmaceuticals. People began engaging in health tourism as a result of their international travels in pursuit of more affordable clinical care or as a means of avoiding being constrained by the records of their own country (Stojanovic, Stojanovic, and Randelovic, 2010).[16]

iv) **Eco-Tourism:** It is environmentally responsible tourism, protecting natural resources and preserving the local community's economy and social standing. Travelers who practise Eco-tourism gravitate to delicate, perfect, and frequently protective regions that aim for minimum impact and frequently have a small scale . It is

---

14 *Spychala, A., Sylwia G. (2013). "What is Nature Tourism? Case Study of University Students". Turyzm, Vol. 1, No.1.*

15 *Mousavi, S. S., Doratli, N., Mousavi, S.N., Moradiahari, F. (2016) "Defining Cultural Tourism", International Conference on Civil, Architecture and Sustainable Development, Vol. 1, No. 1, (December).*

16 *Stojanovic, M., Stojanovic, D., Randelovic, D. (2010). "New Trends in Participation at Tourist Market under Conditions of Global Economic Crisis", Tourism and Hospitality Management, Vo. 1, No. 1.*

a style of tourism that is primarily inspired by a region's natural heritage, especially its indigenous societies (Ziffer, 1989)[17].

v) Home-stay Tourism: The term "home stay" implies, a home stay is a paid stay in a person's home for a brief period of time, with accommodations and other services being given by local communities and families to such guests. Because of this, the Home- Stay Regulation acknowledges that it may be managed by a single individual or by a group of individuals (Timilsina, 2012)[18]. By offering clean, comfortable, and affordable housing and food, home stay tries to draw travelers away from trendy and crowded urban areas and into the rural surrounds, where they may enjoy the lovely scenery. Visitors can engage with the host family while also getting a special cultural experience from a home stay. It motivates people to visit uncharted and novel locations.

I.4. Tourism and Sustainable Development:

The Bruntdland Report (1987)[19] defined sustainable development as "development that meets the needs of the present without compromising the ability of future generations to meet their own needs" (Bruntdland Report, 1987, p. 41). Sustainable development has been categorized from a variety of perspectives.

In his book, 'The Global Possible'[20], Robert Repetto provides a crucial concept of sustainable development. According to him, sustainable development is an ongoing process that takes into account both

17   *Ziffer, A. K. (1989). 'Ecotourism: The Uneasy Alliance', Conservation International, Ernst and Young, Washington D.C.*

18   *Timilsina P (2012) Homestay Tourism Boosts Ghale Gaon's Economy. Retrieved from http://www.gorkhapatra.org.np.*

19   *Brundtland Report (1987); World Commission on Environment and Development*

20   *Repetto, R. (1985); 'The Global Possible: Resources, Development, and the New Century', (World Resources Institute Book), New Haven and London, Yale University Press.*

natural and human resources as a way to accomplish specific goals or objectives. This method of development shouldn't conflict with nature. Instead, it should follow the natural production process, according to Repeto (Repetto, 1985 pp. 47). A process of reconciliation between the majority and, at times, even between generations is what it is and what it should always be. Sustainable development is a developmental idea that lowers poverty and raises living standards for all people, especially those involved in rural tourism. Rural tourism has the ability to contribute to environmental preservation and protection. As a result, all parties involved, including governments, may be conscious of the need to protect the environment and work towards sustainable tourist growth. Sustainable development is typically evaluated using the standard of living in rural areas (Kazana and Kazaklis, 2009).[21] Growth that does not interfere with the biotic and abiotic systems of the earth is referred to as sustainable development. The goal of sustainable tourism is to maintain the overall quality of both people and the environment over time (Reid, 1995)[22].

In the long run, rural tourism helps to make an economy viable. A lifestyle that is both economically viable and sustainable; is referred to as being economically sustainable. As a result, it is important to recognize that rural tourism benefits people's long-term health, entertainment, and education as well as the preservation and protection of the environment. Among other things, it permits the provision of food and beverages. Rural tourism helps a community to maintain its socio-cultural integrity, which includes the sincerity of its interpersonal ties, adherence to customs and rites, as well as its material and emotional way of life. It also discusses the distinctiveness, cultural heritage,

---

21 *Kazana, V., Kazaklis, A. Merou, Th., Takos, I. (2009). 'Fuzzy Multi-Criteria Modelling for Impact Assessment in the Context of Sustainable Forest Management. A Greek Case Study'. In: M. Palahi, Y. Birot, F. Bravo and E. Gorriz (eds), EFI Proceedings 57, pp 175-184*

22 *Reid, D. (1995); 'Sustainable Development: An Introductory Guide', Routledge, London.*

and traditions of the region, which are reflected in the local cuisine, hospitality, social gatherings, vernacular skills, and religious variety (Pizam and Milman, 1986)[23].

The environmental component of rural tourism sustainability is concentrated on highlighting the function of the environment and public perceptions towards it, encouraging environmentally conscious business practices, and reducing tourists' environmental behaviour, measures to minimize, and various methods for energy conservation. It is a technique for improving environmental awareness that can be applied to help to defend the preservation of natural areas while also boosting their economic value. (Sunlu, 2003).[24]

I.5.   Rural Tourism and Sustainable Development:

In many countries, rural areas are less developed than urban areas. They are often perceived as having many problems, such as low productivity, low education, and low income. Other issues include

---

23   *Pizam, A., Milman, A. (1986). "The Social Impacts of Tourism", Tourism Recreation Research, Vol. 11, No. 1*

24   *Sunlu, U. (2003). "Environmental Impacts of Tourism", CIHEAM, Vol. 1, No. 1*

population shifts from rural to urban areas, low economic growth, declining employment opportunities, the loss of farms, impacts on historical and cultural heritage, sharp demographic changes, and low quality of life. These issues indicate that maintaining agricultural activities without change might create deeper social problems in rural regions. Understanding the contributions of rural tourism to rural community development is critical for helping government and community planners to realize whether rural tourism development is beneficial. Policy-makers are aware that reducing rural vulnerability and enhancing rural resilience; is a necessary but a challenging task. Therefore, it is important to consider the equilibrium between rural development and potential negative impacts. For example, economic growth may improve the quality of life and enhance the well-being index. However, it may worsen income inequality, increase the demand for green landscapes, and intensify environmental pollution, and these changes may impede natural preservation in rural regions and make local residents' lives more stressful. This might lead policy-makers to question whether they should support tourism-based rural development. Thus, the provision of specific information on the contributions of rural tourism is crucial for policy-makers. Today, rural tourism has responded to the new demand trends of short-term tourists, directly providing visitors with unique services and opportunities to contact other business channels. Rural tourism no longer refers solely to the benefits of agricultural production; through economic improvement, it represents a greater diversity of activities. It is important to take advantage of the novel social and cultural alternatives offered by rural tourism, which contribute for the development of countryside. For rural tourism to support environmental preservation and sustainable economic growth, development is required. Rural tourism is essential for improving rural livelihoods and promoting the socioeconomic well-being of the populace (Nooripoor et al. (2020)[25]. Rural tourism supports the identities and harmony of the neighborhood as well as the long-term preservation of its sociocultural values and standard of living. Rural tourism boosts inhabitants' sales revenues, which leads to the creation of new farm goods and the sustainable growth of the rural region (Okech et al., 2012)[26]. Development is the most significant factor in rural tourism.

On the other side, rural tourism emphasizes sustainable improvement in terms of the resources needed by both the present and future generations, rather than only development in terms of its altered architecture. Rural tourism and sustainable development go hand in hand in the creation of a new host region, assisting in the planning of scientific resources, commercial success, social and aesthetic fulfilment, and the promotion of traditions and biodiversity. In addition to maximizing potential in the future, they complement one another in addressing the demands of tourism and the host region. Therefore, in the context of rural tourism, sustainable development may be seen as a long-term tourism plan that takes into account the needs of the general public, local residents, tourists, and ultimately the entire tourism industry.

In terms of the local geographical context, two contributions could be made by rural tourism. The first stems from the environmental perspective. When a rural community develops rural tourism, environmental protection awareness is increased, and the responsible utilization of natural resources is promoted.

---

25 *Nooripoor, et al. (2020). "The Role of Tourism in Rural Development: Evidence from Iran", Geo Journal, Vol.1, No.1.*

26 *Okech, et al. (2012). "Rural Tourism as a Sustainable Development Alternative: An Analysis with Special Reference to Luanda, Kenya", Culture, Vol. 3, No.1. (August)*

Monastery (Source: google.com)

I.6. Rural Tourism Destinations and their Potential for Tourism Development:

The term 'tourism potential' refers to something that occurs but has yet to be completely recognized. As a result, it represents the set of descriptive and analytical variables that determine the degree and scope of tourism exploitation in the region. It is challenging to quantify potential in the tourism industry because there are so many aspects to consider (Marvah and Ganguly, 1999). Any natural, cultural, or manmade entity with the potential to attract tourists and lead to development is considered to have tourism potential. As a result, natural landscapes and natural resources such as a river, a mountain, a hill, a waterfall, a lake, wildlife, and historical and cultural sites such as preserved heritage monuments, sculptures, architectures, historic landmarks, and so on, as well as resorts, parks, and other points of interest, can all become potential tourist attractions.

Tourism potential is already reflected in infrastructure and cultural features (Munian Sushani, 2014). Rural tourism potential exists when rural communities' long-term growth is built not only on appealing landscapes and infrastructure but also on competitively priced, high-quality services. Since the region's rural areas have a lot of cultural and historical value rural tourism has a lot of growth potential. Improving infrastructure, historic landmarks, rehabilitating architecture, and encouraging the preservation of the environment in rural regions all benefit the development of rural tourism. Several variables, including the suitable infrastructure, development of different sites, viewpoints, attractions, etc. along with improvement in services, provision of parking facilities, provision of safety and security of tourists leads to tourism development in rural areas. Rural tourism which is an important source of income for the residents should be given special consideration in terms of diversifying rural economic sources.

I.6.1. Rural Tourism Destinations in Darjeeling Himalayas:

Darjeeling Himalaya is a repository of great tourism potential. The rustic mountain hamlets located at the back and beyond the typical hill stations are replete with rich tourism potential. However, inadequate infrastructure and remoteness of most of these places have held them unexplored.

Based on natural tourism potential e.g. landscape relief, climate, hydrologic and biographic conditions, Chatakpur, Lamahatta and Takdah get greater importance since they have beautiful landscapes and pleasant climates. Sittong is a bit warmer. Chatakpur, Lamahatta and Takdah have scenic beauty while Sittong give exposure to pristine locations. In terms of natural potential, it can be said that Chatakpur, Lamahatta and Takdah have an edge over Sittong, but all have firmly established their places on the map of rural tourism in Darjeeling Himalayas.

Destination	Distance from NJP Bagdogra in km. (apprx.)	Time Taken (hours)	Transport Cost
Sittong	78 (via Mungpoo)	3.5	Rs. 500 approx. by shared taxi/ Rs. 3000 approx. by reserved vehicle
Takdah	65 (via Jorebunglow)	3.5	Rs. 500 approx. by shared taxi/ Rs. 3000 approx. by reserved vehicle
Lamahatta	60 (via Jorebunglow)	3	Rs. 500 approx. by shared taxi/ Rs. 3000 approx. by reserved vehicle
Chatakpur	62 (via sonada)	3	Rs. 500 approx. by shared taxi/ Rs. 3000 approx. by reserved vehicle

Table 1.1. Location and Locational Advantages of Different Rural Tourism Destinations

A. **Takdah**, an old British cantonment area started as yearly as in 1900s, is 65 km from NJP railway station (via Jorebunglow) and about 65 km from Bagdogra airport. The journey takes approximately 3.5 hours. The cost is Rs. 500 approx. by shared taxi/ Rs. 3000 approx. by reserved vehicle (as of 2023). Takdah, a quiet and serene place, attracts a lot of tourists from India and abroad. The original name was pronounced as '*Tukdah*' which is derived from Lepcha word means 'mist' / 'fog', and in a true sense the area is covered with fog in majority of days in a year. The meandering road, chirping of birds, the scenic views, the nature trails through the forests make the journey beautiful and provide the traveler immense pleasure. The condition of the road is good. All-weather roads make it easy and comfortable for travelers. Except for traffic jams at Jorebunglow, the rest of the road remains open. There are numbers of Private homestays are available for the tourists to enjoy their vacations in a peaceful manner.

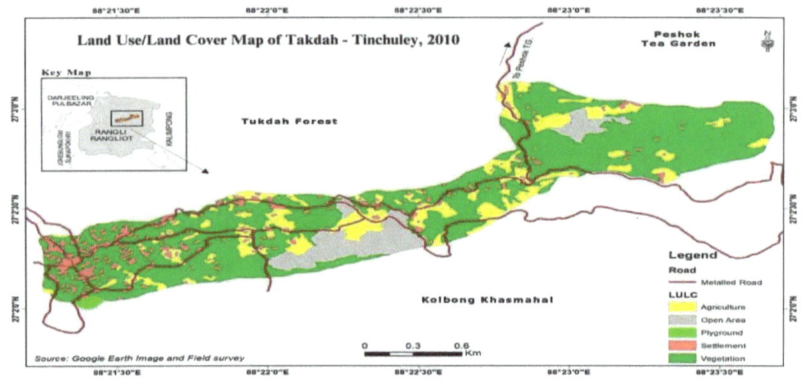

Land use/Land cover Map showing the development of infrastructure and homestays at Takdah from 2010 to 2023

Heritage Bungalow No12. Source: google.com

B. **Lamahatta,** a small village, is 60 km from NJP railway station (via Jorebunglow) and about 60 km from Bagdogra airport is only 23 kms far from Darjeeling. Surrounded by beautiful scenic view of Mt. Kanchenjunga, this picturesque village has been developed as eco-tourism destination in late 2012.

The place is an altitude of 6800 ft, is a calm and peaceful place with pine trees standing majestically with parks and well maintained gardens. The Lamahatta tour offers a quiet, serene and romantic atmosphere along the forest road. The beautiful metallic road makes for a fun trip to Lamahatta. Roads and the rest of the places are open except for traffic congestion at Jorebunglow.

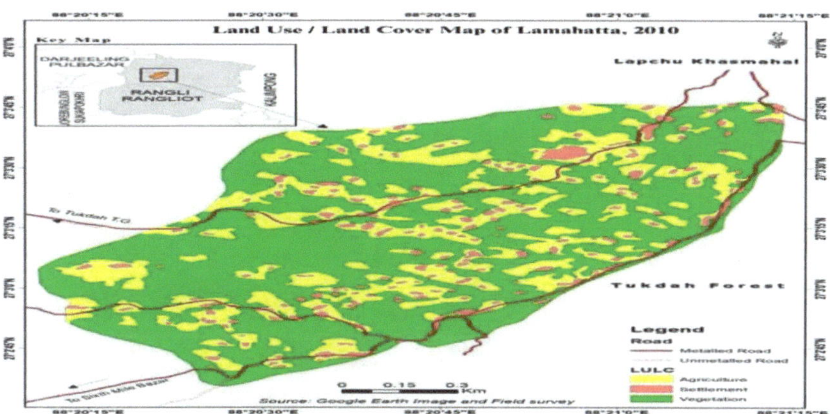

Land use / Land cover Map showing the development of infrastructure and homestays at Lamahatta from 2010 to 2023

Source: google.com

C. **Chatakpur**, a tiny forest village near Sonada is 62 km from NJP railway station (via Ghoom) and more or less 62 km from Bagdogra airport. This forest village is located 7 kms from Sonada amidst the Senchal Reserve forest of Eastern Himalayas, at an elevation of 7887 ft. Chatakpur is entered through dense pine forests, oaks, and rhododendrons, providing a calm and peaceful environment. The rough road makes a thrilling trip to Chatakpur. Chatakpur is mainly inhabited by tribal communities. It provides a panoramic view of snow-capped mountains of the Himalayan range. October to February is the best period to visit with snow falls during the winter season. In a clear sunny day, one can view Mt. Kanchanjunga better than any other place with chirping of birds and the strange sounds of animals.

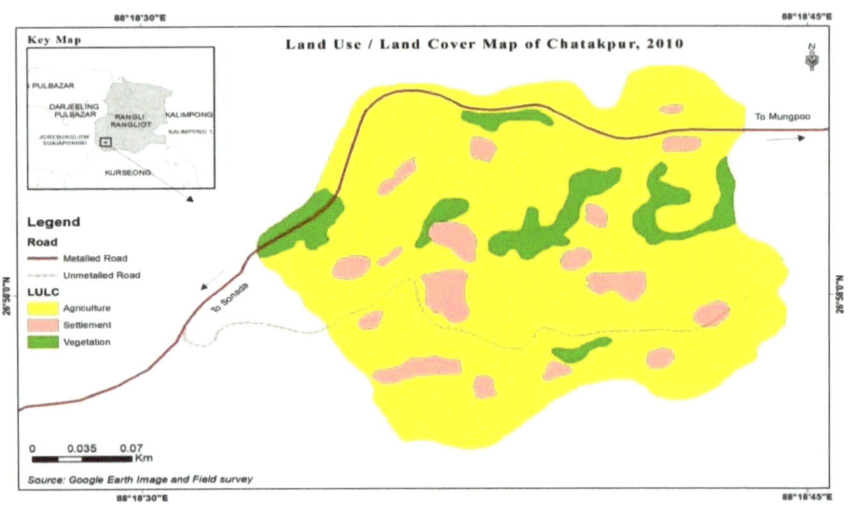

Land use / Land cover Map showing the development of infrastructure and homestays at Chatakpur from 2010 to 2023

Source: google.com

D. **Sittong**, a quaint Lepcha hamlet, is beneficial to the growth of rural tourism surrounded by luxuriant orange orchard, perched at an altitude of 4000ft. With a rich cultural and historical potential and huge agricultural areas, there is indeed a significant deal of cultural and natural diversity. The environment, as well as local customs and identity, have been effectively preserved. In addition, the rural areas of the Darjeeling Himalaya have a relatively high tourism potential due to favourable conditions, beautiful landscapes, presence of natural resources, pleasant climate, good infrastructure and precious religious and cultural heritage. Sittong, a horticulture village is 78 km from NJP railway station (via Ghoom) and about 78 km from Bagdogra airport. The journey to this forest village needs around 3.5 hours. The journey towards Sittong offers a calm and peaceful atmosphere through pine forests and rich orange gardens. The well-metalized roads to Sittong give the tourists pleasure and a happy journey.

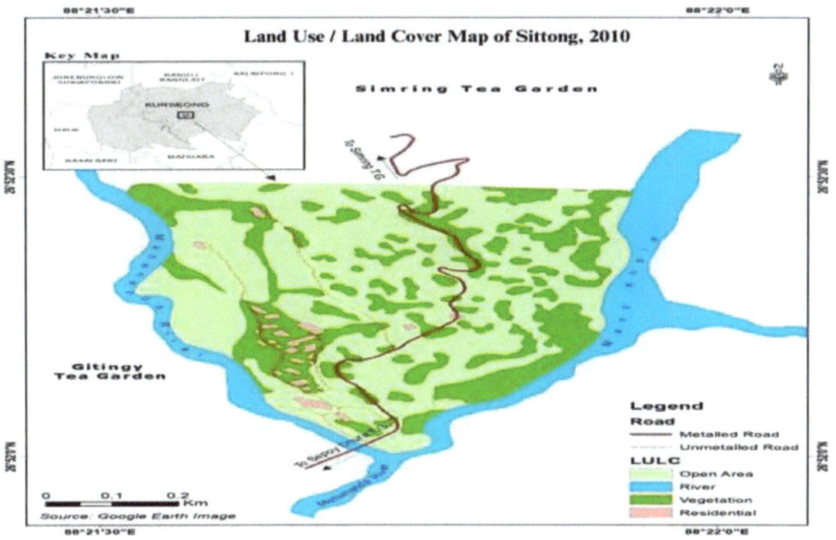

Land use / Landcover Map showing the development of infrastructure and homestays at Sittong from 2010 to 2023

Source: google.com

The Darjeeling Himalayas possesses natural potential as a rural tourism destination, such as various terrain configurations, breath- taking landscapes, geographical representation by flora and fauna, good weather conditions and clean water and air.

Chapter - II

Research Methodology

The current study uses approaches that are descriptive, analytical, comparative, interpretative and evaluative. Both qualitative and quantitative data were employed in the study. To collect primary data, a structured interviewing procedure was used with travelers, tourism industry professionals, and local stakeholders. A standardized questionnaire was distributed to the locals to get their comments. Secondary data were collected using prior studies in tourism, rural tourism and ecotourism, as well as publications from the tourism departments of India and Darjeeling, as well as a variety of journals, publications, magazines, newspapers and management plans for national parks and wildlife sanctuaries. By visiting specified websites and online portals, more data were collected and analysed.

Four rural tourism destinations have been chosen based on their popularity, accessibility, tranquilly of the surroundings and overall influence on the hosts' and guests' quality of life. These are Chatakpur & Sittong from the Kurseong Sub-division and Takdah & Lamahatta from the Darjeeling Sub-division. Different questionnaires were prepared for tourists, homestay owners and their families and locals for content analysis using both organised, unstructured patterns, close-ended and open-ended questions. Methods of stratified random sampling have been used for this.

Additionally, observations, interviews, and photographs have been taken to investigate in detail the pattern of development of tourism, the factors that played a crucial role in its high points and low points, the socioeconomic aspects of tourists and homestay owners, the impact that tourists have on the local community, the economic impact of rural tourism, the difficulties that this particular sector has been facing, and the future prospects. With field visits, internal data commitment has been ensured. From the information sheets, summary tables have been created, and they have been controlled using both appropriate subjective and quantitative procedures. By using MS Excel and GIS software, the study's findings have been handled, analysed, and rendered as tables, charts, graphs, diagrams, and maps that adhere to accepted cartographic standards. For mapping and comparing development, Arc GIS 10 was used and SPSS 23 was used for data analysis.

In the chosen rural tourism destinations of the Darjeeling Himalayas, a pilot survey was carried out to distinguish the techniques, indicators, sample size, and stakeholders. Four major rural tourist places were chosen in the Darjeeling Himalaya to better understand the potential of rural tourism as a tool for sustainable development: Takdah, Lamahatta, Chatakpur, and Sittong.

Evaluating rural tourism's long-term viability required measurements of its effects on the economy, society, history, and environment. Economic, social, cultural, and environmental indices were utilised to assess the effects of rural tourism in the Darjeeling Himalaya. Three different stakeholder groups actively participating in Darjeeling Himalaya's rural tourism initiatives provided the primary data sources. A questionnaire was used to gather primary data from tourists as well. To examine the perceptions of homestay owners, a total of 40 respondents were chosen at random. A total of 80 respondents (20 samples from each site) were used to explore the perspectives of locals, and 280 respondents (70 samples from each destination) were used to analyse tourists' perceptions. 50 respondents were chosen at random to participate in the evaluation of authorities who were directly or indirectly involved with ecotourism. Focus group discussions, individual interviews, and pre-tested questionnaires were the main methods used to gather the primary data. These stakeholders were gathered through three rounds of interviews, and a 5-point Likert scale was used to assess the sustainability of Darjeeling Himalaya's rural tourism. The accompanying tables are used to explain the subtleties of sampling.

An extensive review of the literatures revealed the various influences on economic, sociocultural, and environmental growth. For the purpose of gathering primary data, a structured questionnaire schedule was created using the knowledge gained from the literature research. Then, using tables and a 5-point Likert scale with responses ranging from Strongly Agree (5) to Agree (4) to Neutral (3) to Disagree (4) to Strongly Disagree (5) a study of tourists, guesthouse owners, and locals was attempted.

To learn more about the types of tourists who visit rural areas and their satisfaction levels, a structured questionnaire was employed. The five 'A's' of rural tourism—attraction, accommodation, accessibility, amenities and awareness—as well as other factors on a Likert scale of 1 to 5 have been examined. The level of satisfaction of all visitors, both domestic and foreign, with the various amenities they enjoyed having available at each of the four rural tourism destinations have been analysed. These amenities include lodging, infrastructure (transport), food, services, attitudes of people, culture, the location's draw, shopping, parking, cleanliness, drinking water, how the locals treat visitors and the scenic beauty and so on and so forth. A 5-point Likert scale with the options Very Satisfactory, Satisfactory, Neutral, Unsatisfactory and Very Unsatisfactory was used to poll 280 visitors evaluating the amenities.

II.1. Areas of Study:

The locations for case study on rural tourism included Takdah & Lamahatta, from the Darjeeling Sub-division as well as Chatakpur & Sittong from the Kurseong Sub-division.

II.2. Objectives of Study:

Based on the analysis presented above, the objectives of the present research were:

i) Understanding the rural tourism situation in the Darjeeling Himalayas.

ii) Identifying the nature and rate of growth of rural tourism in the study area.

iii) Examining the geographic factors influencing rural tourism and its benefits in the study area.

iv) Examining the potentials and opportunities for rural tourism in the study area.

v) Analyzing the effects of rural tourism and visitor behaviour in the study area.

vi) To determine the challenges and opportunities for further research into and development of rural tourism in the study area.

vii) To analyze the diverse challenges of rural tourism in the study area.

II.3. Review of Literatures:

a. Review on Tourism:

Pearce (1980) in his article "Host Community Acceptance of Foreign Tourists: Strategic Considerations" contends that extensive tourism development may aggravate congestion in areas along with safety issues, violence, pricing, and other factors among residents. However, it is self-evident that closer proximity by all tourism industries means more significant economic development and larger revenues for the locals. As a result, in addition to raising environmental awareness, it may also encourage high regard concerning the tourism business, which is a growing source of cash for the area.

Sharma (1985) investigated the socio-economic relevance of tourism in his paper "Tourism: Its Socio-Economic Importance" in Southern Economist. Remarkably, the tourism industry has grown to be considered as a catalyst for monetary development as well as a powerful tool for social healing and currency conversion opportunities. He considers the tourism sector's financial importance, which he compares to its commitment to wage growth, fresh foreign earnings, work, profitability, and asset protection.

Var, Sheldon, and Liu (1987) analyzed "Resident Perceptions of the Environmental Impacts of Tourism" as a capacity that is legitimately reliant on the proportion between the number of tourists and the number of residents. The findings show that regardless of the physical location or level of tourism maturity, all residents of a country are affected by tourism.

Murti and Kumar (1989) in their book, 'Tourists Activities Causing Depletion of Plant Wealth in Jammu & Kashmir, India: Impacts of Tourism on Mountain Environment' pointed out that the subject of tourist numbers in the tourism sector is inextricably linked to preservation difficulties. They discover that the tourism sector is integrated into pilgrimage zones such as Vaishnodevi and Amarnath as well as adventure in different popular tourism destinations such as Sonamarg, Pahalgam and Gulmarg. As a result, such delicate excellence zones must be entirely secured after reaching their voyager transporting limit, so that their natural framework and natural landscapes operations are not imperiled.

Negi (1990) in his book, 'Tourism and Travel' features the attractions of rural areas, which incorporate satisfaction in the country landscape, the craving for open space, provincial games like fishing, chasing, and ethnic attractions like social life, custom, food, beverages, and celebrations. The article additionally expresses that rural tourism could incorporate delicate farms and fields of lowland rural areas and fields, slopes and mountains of rough terrain rural areas along with rural areas developed in coastal sides.

Martin and McCool (1992) in their study "Attitude of Montana Residents towards Tourism Development, Missoula" founded that residents fear that they might be driven out of nearby primary activities and other recreational areas as the tourism sector grows. However, the vast majority of such studies either never provide experimental evidence that increasing tourist volumes in a network leads to more unfavourable attitudes, or simply confine the research to instructive ambient assessments of mentalities in a single platform or place.

Panda, Mishra and Parida (1992), in the book entitled 'Tourism Management - The Socio-Economic and Ecological Perspective', analyzed that from a single perspective, natural and man-made resources are essential components in the construction of the tourism sector. Contrary to this, tourism may harm the environment, resulting in a variety of adverse and unintended consequences.

Stettner (1993) in his article "Community or commodity? Sustainable Development in Mountain Resorts" emphasized the approach which can be beneficial in improving the tourist industry and its impact on the local community in a reasonable manner. The tourist industry must be built to preserve the unique traits of the sights and residents that will aim to receive guests for the long term. As a result, the hill tourism link may prove to be a true paradigm of sustainable development for global reach.

Pandya and Oza (1994) in their study entitled "Biodiversity for the Masses" emphasize the necessity of natural resources protection and its economic utilization. People should know their responsibility to protect different species and create a pattern of harmony with the environment. They suggest that before the last chance is lost, awareness should be made among the public, primarily the young generation, different stakeholders, and different governmental as well as private agencies.

Chettri (1998) in his article entitled "Impact of Tourism on Biodiversity" analyzes that the beginning of restoration practices has really been prepared by the systems, and has actively undertaken works on resources and rich biodiversity observation. It is critical to look for specific specialties that rely on certain local species mostly for the important aspects of life that is ammunition, forage, and forestry to preserve the region's biodiversity. Michael and Addison (1999) in their book 'Sustainable Tourism - A Geographical Perspective', focus on the long-term benefits of ecotourism and express that ecotourism is naturally benevolent and manageable tourism that additionally benefits the nearby network. Numerous ecotourism adventures obliterate the very biological systems they guarantee to secure. They fear that with a lack of prudence, ecotourism winds up in ecological corruption.

Rajan and Thankappan (2001) in their article "Impact of Tourism on the Environment of Munnar" suggest that the proper implementation of eco-tourism activities can bring challenges to light as well as a need for preservation, which can greatly contribute to the ecological security and reverence of any region. They claim that uncontrolled regular tourism poses a significant risk to the biological system. Munnar, for example, requires an acceptable critical arrangement for practical and capable tourist development that includes travel industry exercises focusing on the protection of normal assets, circumstances, and respect for adjacent cultures and customs.

Gursoy, Jurowski, and Uysal (2002) in their study "Resident's Attitudes: A Structural Modelling Approach" directed a review to present a good network of tourist residents and stakeholders and to support tourism, based on the components discovered to an effective response to its turn of events. The findings revealed that the residents' contribution plays an important role in the development of society with the use of tourism assets and a positive attitude towards tourists. Rao (2002) in his article "Challenges and Issues for Tourism in the South Pacific Island States: The Case of the Fiji Islands" has investigated the difficulties concerning tourism. He suggested that the government institutions should recognize tourism's role as an economic generator and the most important source of foreign commerce. The tourism sector can be improved if the difficulties of stakeholders are reduced. He warns that a carefully crafted travel sector development strategy may have detrimental effects on the country rather than contributing to its advancement. Kohli (2002) in his article "Ecotourism and Himalayas" argues that ecotourism can enhance residents' livelihood and can bring regional development without harming the environment if proper methods are applied. Various awareness programs should be implemented. The enhancement of ecotourism by ensuring the condition of numerous sorts of trees and plants exasperates the great perfection of the Himalayas.

Sethi (2002) in the book entitled, 'Millennium Trends in Travel and Tourism' expressed that selling various tourism items to international tourists is an excellent way to earn foreign exchange. The converse is true in terms of tourism spending. The domestic tourists and the locals use different locations to buy different tourism packages investing very little as compared to foreign tourists. As a result, both local and international tourists are critical to the tourism industry.

Liu (2003) in his article "Sustainable Tourism Development: A Critique" examines the flaws in sustainable development. He believes that diverse stakeholders, governments, and scholars should pay attention to the function of tourist demand, the form of tourism products, tourism's support of socio-cultural advancement, and various types of sustainability. He also suggests that various agencies execute different policies in practice.

Tosun and Timothy (2003) investigate the grounds of ineffective tourist improvement at the local level in their article "Arguments for Community Participation in the Tourism Development Process". The tourism industry can grow only if the local community participates in different activities of tourism and contributes to the development of society. However, some factors that resulted in unsustainable tourism growth have been discovered to be beyond the capability or influence of indigenous individuals in the organization.

Perez and Nadal (2005) in their study "Host Community Perceptions" conducted group investigation methods to assess how residents perceive the tourist sector as shaping their environment. Their findings demonstrate that participants are aware of the favourable as well as adverse effects of tourism, thus participants are divided on an improvement proposition with growing vacationers. Furthermore, it shows that some progression strategies create severe restoration resistance, while others benefit from common assistance.

Badan and Bhatt (2006) in their book entitled, 'Sustainable Tourism' examined and evaluated the methods whereby the systems can efficiently and successfully promote tourism by properly monitoring its progress such that it introduces the benefits that the system desires while restricting its unfavourable impacts. Though the tourism industry offers huge opportunities for earning capital, the local people should be aware of its adverse effects. The government must work out ways to keep the tourism business commercially sustainable.

Aneja (2006) in his article "Sustainable Tourism Development Challenges Ahead" describes a feasible tourist industry that tries to solve the present stakeholders' and tourists' problems ensuring long-term socio-economic benefits from tourism. All the stakeholders and tourists involved in tourism activities should cope with the challenges positively without harming the environment. Lepp (2007) in his article "Inhabitants' Attitudes towards Tourism in Bigodi Village, Uganda" has brought up the occupant's mentalities towards the travel industry and discovers that occupants have reliably inspirational perspectives towards tourism. Uplifting mentalities result from the inhabitant's conviction that tourism makes network advancement, improves horticultural markets, creates pay, lastly, that the travel industry brings irregular favourable luck.

Bhattacharya (2008) in his article "Tourism Development in Northeast India: Changing Recreational Demand, Developmental Challenges and Issues associated with Sustainability" believed that the tourism industry needs to embrace a long-term tourism development plan. Effective marketing can enhance the region's current socio-economic position, given the region's cultural richness and biological and socio-cultural resources. Because the area is not really in a position to provide a better tourist experience, therefore, successful management and execution of the tourist industry in this geographical area will necessitate efficient performance at the local level.

Nomani and Khan (2015) in their article "Human Resource Development in Tourism Industry –An Analytical Framework" have discussed the role of tourism on human asset advancement. On the off chance that the travel industry prospers in India, the nation will have monetary addition. They propose that Human resource development methodologies ought to concentrate on maintainability-based industry rehearses, the travel industry improvement, esteem frameworks, and standards of conduct among all the partners.

Akihito (2017) in his article "Advancement of Tourism and the Tourist Industry in India: A Case Study of Uttarakhand", expressed that the broadening of ways of life that go with a thriving working- class has empowered the improvement of the tourism industry as a relaxation action. He proposes that there are significant advantages that can be considered typical from the inundation of sightseers if there are upgrades in the frontage roads that interface significant parkways with housing facilities.

Subsequently, a specific gradually expanding influence on the nearby economy can be noticed for both local inhabitants and traders inside the locale for work at housing facilities, vital administrations, and the interest for materials.

Goyal (2018) in his article "Economic Aspects of Tourism in India", stated that movement and tourism are significant monetary actions in many nations around the planet. Indian tourism has been developing at a quick speed and has displayed a tremendous potential for producing business, procuring unfamiliar trade along these lines elevating the economy. He analyses that tourism has contributed massively to the prospering diagram of India's economy by pulling in countless both unfamiliar and home-grown tourists. He discovers that tourism in India has had the option to create a business, acquire unfamiliar trade, and get foundation improvement, and increment government income.

b. **Review on Eco-tourism:**

Singh (1997) in his article "Ecotourism and Environmental Conservation in India" endeavoured to learn about various aspects of ecotourism and various techniques followed for the preservation of the environment. He opines that all ecotourism areas should be well preserved and protected by the authorities, residents and the tourists themselves. Ecotourism can be improved if an adequate measure of exertion is given on growing new interventions and procedures in rural areas. As eco-tourism is environment-friendly, the conservation measures should not only come from the government but also all the stakeholders involved in ecotourism sectors.

Henderson, et al. (2001) in their article "Urban Environmental and Nature-Based Attractions: Green Tourism in Singapore" discussed how nature-based tourism attracts both domestic and international visitors. They've discovered that the green travelers of the 21st century may be happy with advantageous and available normal attractions, which offer some benefit for cash, wellbeing and security.

Bande (2005) in her article "Eco-Tourism and Mountains" brought up that ecotourism represents the administration of the travel industry in such a way, that man gets the greatest advantages from nature without upsetting its intrinsic equalization. It looks to re- establish man's correspondence with nature, satisfying their need without upsetting the nearby culture and convention.

Gale and Hil (2009) in the book entitled "Ecotourism and Environmental Sustainability- Principles and Practice" witnessed the brilliant connection between tourist industries with nature. Ecotourism is such a paradigm that vacationers are increasingly looking for in the travel business. Manufactured stocks, agricultural landmasses, and surface mining and quarrying have all been discussed concerning ecotourism.

Jalania (2012) in his article "Nearby People's Perception on the Impacts and Importance of Ecotourism in Sabang, Palawan, Philippines", investigated the effects of eco-tourism on work age and individual inundation. He claimed that the tourism business has been able to provide jobs for the villagers. While ecotourism benefits residents in some ways, ecological sustainability has seen the least amount of beneficial consequences in terms of job opportunities and city progress.

Kiper (2013) in his article "Role of Ecotourism in Sustainable Tourism" expressed that Eco-tourism is a compelling instrument for the manageable turn of events and is the motivation behind why nations are presently grasping it and remembering it for their financial turn of events and protection procedures. Ecotourism must record for social, financial, and natural ramifications, to succeed. Ecotourism helps in network advancement by giving the substitute wellspring of jobs to neighbourhood networks, which is more feasible.

Postica and Cardoso (2014) in their article "Current Development Level of Ecotourism and Eco-Touristic Products in Moldova" looked at the front line situation and improvement phase of ecotourism in Moldova and viewpoints ecotourism as a limit technique to ensure common biological systems and simultaneously to advance practical local improvement. Ecotourism is a creating region of premium commercial centre inside the enormous visit industry with the limit of being a pivotal economic advancement device. Ecotourism as a commercial centre area is essential for nature tourism and has more intense connections to country and social tourism.

Vishwanatha and Chandrashekara (2014) in their article "A Study on the Environmental Impacts of Ecotourism in Kodagu District, Karnataka" had examined the positive and negative ecological effects of eco-tourism. As specified, the absence of information and mindfulness in individuals will affect ecotourism. Consequently, stakeholders and concerned specialists should work on this issue to the sincere and manageable improvement of eco-tourism.

Bassam and Rahman (2016) in their article "Social Impacts of Eco-tourism in India" focused on the handiness of investigation of eco-tourism and understanding the issues and prospects of ecotourism in India which help to advance economic improvement by increasing expectations of living with incredible natural assurance. They propose that ecotourism ought to be nature-based and biologically feasible including fitting re-visitations of the local area and long haul protection of assets. They further propose that the incorporated natural, social, and financial arranging investigation ought to be attempted before the initiation of any significant activities.

Tripathi and Jain (2017) in their article "Openings and Challenges of Ecotourism concerning its Employability Potential: Uttar Pradesh, India", had observed that ecotourism has procured much interest in current years, especially in non-industrial nations. It fulfills the local area's desires for occupations, generates employment, and enhances new capabilities, and the work and better status of women. It moreover desires to prepare and provide information to the tourists, offers measurements and money for the preservation of nature, carries out direct preferred position to the financial improvement and political strengthening of local networks and zones, and cultivates respect for exceptional societies and common freedoms.

Mishra (2019) in his article "Analysing the Prospect of Sustainable Eco and Rural Tourism in Purulia District of West Bengal", found that the exertion of local area strengthening is treated as a compelling instrument for reverse zone advancement plans prompting controlling the size of the difference. He further talks about the significance and probability of presenting ecotourism and rural tourism towards achieving more prominent local area strengthening with regards to review perceptions on the interaction of change of country work in the forestland of the western part, especially the region of Purulia, of West Bengal - the centre of present decentralized plans and the prohibition of the nearby networks in dynamic cycles.

Saidmamatov et al. (2020) in their article "Utilizing Ecotourism Opportunities for Sustainability in the Aral Sea Region: Prospects and Challenges" observed the administrators' mindfulness on advantages of advancing ecotourism in the district can diminish biological emergency and prompts feasible turn of events. They talk about their partner's knowledge about ecotourism's worth and are inspired to execute ecotourism in the district on one hand yet, on the other hand, they have restricted perception, skill, and worldwide organizations to advance and market ecotourism items and administrations. A wide scope of advantages can be harvested from creating ecotourism, including work, pay time, and the capacity to improve individuals' lives in nearby networks.

Rai (2020) in her article on "Eco-tourism Potential in the Darjeeling Hills: Prospects, Challenges and Possibilities" found that eco-tourism in the Himalayan district has the rich potential to prosper and improve the economic state of the resident population. However, the travel industry in the district is by all accounts saturated and has made extreme tension on the adjoining resources. To disperse this unfortunate pressing factor, tourists must be channelized away from the saturated metropolitan Darjeeling town to its rural areas. Luckily, as of late, even tourists have begun investigating the rural areas. Her investigations suggested that with the new presentation of practical rural tourism in certain zones, the locals have noticed improved foundation and vocation openings.

c. **Review on Rural Tourism:**

Bojnec (2010) in his article "Rural Tourism, Rural Economy Diversification, and Sustainable Development" explored different trends concerning diversification in the rural economy, to achieve environmental and economic sustainability. He further analyses that rural tourism development is based entirely on remarkable aspects such as a diverse range of environmental endowments, landscape and socio-cultural elements, which benefit the local growth and rural economy.

Dimitrovski (2011) in his article "Rural Tourism and Regional Development: Case Study of the Development of Rural Tourism in the Region of Gruza, Serbia" found that the region has immense opportunities for tourism planning due to its environmental elegance as well as heritage monuments and that if these things are preserved and developed, along with effective government's role in tourism promotion and development, the entire region will progress. According to the findings of his survey, the average tourist stays at a higher socio-economic and cultural level, with the majority of visitors coming from urban regions to enjoy the serenity and natural beauty of rural places.

Katoch and Gautam (2015) in their article "Rural Tourism as a Medium for Local Development in Himachal Pradesh: The example of Villages around Dharamsala (Kangra)" talked about the country individuals' comprehension of the need for provincial tourism and its improvement just as its ensuing advantages to the townspeople around Dharamsala. The town's people know about the advantages of tourism, however, they have almost no comprehension of rural tourism and country tourism approaches executed by the state just as focal government.

Chadha and Choudhary (2016) in their article "Nature, Problems and Prospects of Rural Tourism in Punjab: An Analysis" observed that the tourism industry has become a significant and indispensable piece of economic, social, cultural and actual advancement on the whole agricultural nations. The rural countries, explicitly, advance the travel industry as a strategy for making a new exchange, growing work openings, drawing being created capital, extending government pay, and improving monetary opportunity. Other than being an instrument for creating business openings, the tourism industry has enormous linkages with various territories like cultivating, development, poultry, meticulous work, and advancement, and so forth. Consequently, it creates more comprehensive development.

Manoj (2016) in his article entitled "Impact of Rural Tourism on the Environment and Society: Evidence from Kumbalangi in Kerala, India", witnessed rural tourism from the viewpoint of the nearby network individuals. Rural tourism has given advantages to the neighbourhood network and the conduct of sightseers towards the nearby individuals has been empowering. It has additionally been called attention to the unfavourable impacts of country tourism on the general public and condition, which thus may antagonistically influence its maintainability over the long haul.

Sharma and Parkash (2018) in their article "Rural Tourism in India: Challenges and Opportunities" examined how the various sorts of tourist item expansions impact the improvement prospects of rural areas in India. The public authority should support private areas to advance the tourism industry in rural areas. They further inspect how rural residents can be associated with rural tourism to improve their financial condition. They proposed that the extension of rural tourism and advancement in India can help decrease neediness and improve financial conditions. They proposed that the administration of India should promote rural tourism as a motor of development.

Thathera (2018) in his article "Rural Tourism and Sustainable Development in India" discusseed another sort of development in rural areas related to the rural economy which can convey financial and social benefits to the overall population. He indicates that rural tourism will arise as a significant instrument for feasible improvement including natural assurance, destitution easing, business age, and advancement of distant regions.

II.4.   Data Collection Procedures:

The data were collected on the rural tourism of Darjeeling Himalayas and ways, procedure of tourist in the rural areas. Quantitative data were collected from the four major tourist destinations in Darjeeling Himalayas that is Chattakpur, Lamahatta, Takdah and Sittong. The primary data were collected from direct interaction with a villagers during household survey through questionnaire.

The few data collection method that were used in the survey were:

i)   Data Analysis

ii)   Qualitative Research

iii)   Survey Methodology

iv)   Interviews / questionnaire

II.5.   Sample Size:

The sample size that obtained from the rural tourism of Darjeeling Himalayas was 100. Hundred observations were used to determine estimation of the population of Darjeeling Himalayas. The size of the sample has been drawn from the population itself. The hundred samples that were taken from the Darjeeling Himalayas influenced to statistical properties namely:

a.   The precision of the estimates.

b.   The power of the studies so it could draw conclusions.

The sample size selection was depended on the limited resources as the primary research. The Research questions focused on the size of a parameter and the survey collected sufficient data to have an estimation with a desire level of accuracy of the rural tourism of Darjeeling Himalayas. The tools and techniques that were used in the research were the questionnaire, interview, rating, analysis, interpretation and organisation of data.

II.5.1. Methodology for Assessing Rural Tourism Potential:

Tourism potential in all of Darjeeling Himalaya's rural tourism destinations has been assessed based on two factors: natural potential and anthropogenic potential. All rural tourism destinations' location factors, especially the natural, cultural, and historical components of tourism, were examined. The tourism potential of four rural tourism places in Darjeeling Himalayas, namely Takdah, Lamahatta, Chatakpur, and Sittong, have been assessed using the methods mentioned above.

II.6. Research Gap:

The review of various works of writing on rural tourism and sustainable development reveals that a substantial number of studies on rural tourism and sustainable development in various parts of the world have been conducted. Despite Darjeeling's international reputation as a major tourist destination, no significant or visible work has been done on the Darjeeling Himalayas. Only few studies are available; mostly on the rise, sustainability and significance of the region's rural tourism. In the Darjeeling hills, empirical research on rural tourism's influence from the perspective of sightseers is virtually non-existent. To close the gap, this research was empirically grounded and had included a critical evaluation of rural tourism in the Darjeeling Himalayas.

Chapter - III

Profile of the Study Area: Economic Development and Sustainibility of the Rural Tourism

III.1. Introduction:

The northernmost district in the Indian state of West Bengal, located at the base of the Himalayas, is Darjeeling. The region is well- known for its hill resorts and Darjeeling tea. District administration is located in Darjeeling. The district may be broadly separated between the plains and the hills from a geographic perspective. The Gorkhaland Territorial Administration, a semi-autonomous administrative entity under the state government of West Bengal, oversees the whole district's steep terrain. This group includes the districts of Kalimpong and the three hill subdivisions of Darjeeling, Kurseong, and Mirik. The Terai is the name for the Darjeeling Himalayas' foothills, which are part of the Darjeeling district. The district is bounded on the north by Sikkim, on the south by Kishanganj district of Bihar state, on the southeast by Panchagarh district of Bangladesh, on the east by Kalimpong and Jalpaiguri districts, and on the west by easternmost Province No. 1 of Nepal. Darjeeling district has a length from north to south of 18 miles (29 km) and a breadth from east to west of 16 miles (26 km). As of 2011, it was the second least populous district of West Bengal (out of 19), after Dakshin Dinajpur.

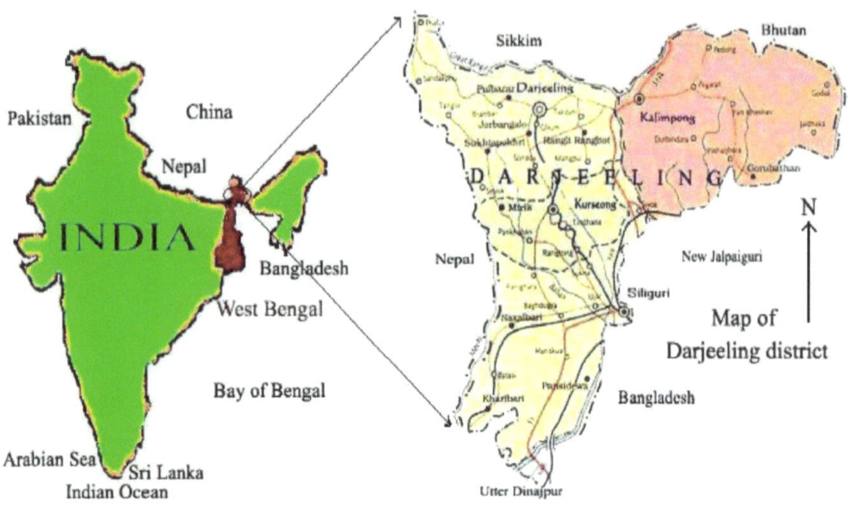

III.2. Study Area:

The northern most district in West Bengal is Darjeeling. It is situated on the Himalayas' southern flank. The district is divided into three subdivisions: Siliguri, Kurseong, and Darjeeling Sadar. The Darjeeling Himalaya is a section of the eastern Himalayan mountains and is bordered to the north, west and east by Sikkim, Nepal and Bhutan respectively. Siliguri is primarily distinguished by the Tarai and district foothills, while it comprises of the first three subdivisions of the district. As a result, Siliguri is excluded from the study in the report. Darjeeling Himalayas covers around 1721 square kilo metres of the district's 3202 square km total territory. The Darjeeling Himalaya is made up of a section of the lower Himalayas' outlying hills and a region known as the Terai that runs along the base of the hills. The Terai is just 91 metres above sea level, 62 although other districts have elevations as high as 3660 metres at Sandakpu. The location has gained the moniker of "Queen of the Hill Stations" due to the breathtaking natural beauty and rejuvenating environment (Chakraborti, P.K 1989)[27]. The Rammam and Rangit are two significant tributaries of the River Teesta, which is the dominant

---

27 *ibid*

stream in the region. Additionally, during the rainy season, various rivulets in the hills that are nourished by rain take on a dominant role in regulating the eco-system. In contrast to the tea plantations that brought prominence to the Darjeeling Himalaya, tourism is a climate-based sector. Darjeeling's climate is particularly notable. The two seasons that tourists choose the most are spring and fall. While the winter following December is excessively chilly and uncomfortable, the monsoon is a time of constant rain. In actuality, the elevation and aspect have a significant impact on the local climate. The first access of the man in the Darjeeling Hills and when who fell down the first tree to establish a living has not clearly been brought to book. But when the British arrived, there were only a small number of people living here among the untouched flora and animals, in a completely natural habitat. Four rural tourism destinations, namely Takdah, Lamahatta, Chatakpur and Sittong have been selected from across Darjeeling Himalayas based on aesthetics and pristine location.

In Darjeeling Sadar subdivision of the Darjeeling district, West Bengal, India, Takdah Cantonment is a suburb. It is part of the Rangli Rangliot CD block, one of the Darjeeling Hills' newest tourist destinations. The name, 'Takdah' literally translates to "always covered" and it is a lovely & charming location in Darjeeling where one may spend out with family and friends.

The major town of Darjeeling is 23 kilometres distant from the little village of Lamahatta, which is situated at an elevation of around 5,700 feet. This charming town, which is surrounded by a pine forest and has a stunning view of Mount Kanchenjunga, was transformed into an eco-tourism destination in late 2012.Lamahatta is a tiny village that mostly relies on farming and cattle raising for its livelihood, although it is well connected to other areas, thanks to the Darjeeling-Kalimpong state route. The park and the well-kept garden inside the community are Lamahatta's main draws. A walking path has also been constructed that will take visitors through a forest of pine trees to two charming ponds known as "jore pokhari" (twin ponds) in the area.

The settlement of Chatakpur Forest is not distant from Darjeeling Town. Although it is just approximately 25 miles from Darjeeling town, getting there might take up to two hours. The reason is because it takes around 10 kilometres to get here by driving through a deep forest in the Senchal region. Chatakpur hamlet is situated on the hill just behind the well-known Tiger Hill of Darjeeling and the village is on the very top of the hill, providing a panoramic view of the surroundings. There are numbers of tourist attractions in Chatakpur. It's a spot where one may appreciate nature and the view of the stunning mountain range. There are just approximately 25 dwellings in the hilltop community, which has a population of roughly 100 people. At the base of the settlement, there is a woodland hut lying on the ground. This used to be a well-liked destination for travellers to stay.

The coordinates of Sittong are 26.93662°N 88.36736°E. The orange-growing region of Darjeeling is home to the hamlet of Sittong. The Riyang River Valley is where it is. Mahananda Wildlife Sanctuary is 13 km from Mangpu. The Sittong region is well known for its orange farming; throughout the winter, the land is completely covered with orange groves. The gardens and their products are quite alluring to tourists. Around Sittong, there are several camping and hiking options. Several hike routes leave from Sittong and travel to different locations.

III.3.   Importance of the Study Area:

A thorough examination of the many social, economic and political advancements that the region has made is necessary to give its underdeveloped socio-economy, politics and infrastructure as well as the variances among these factors within the region. Secondly, the region should be concerned simply because of its geostrategic location. Due to its exposed location, the Darjeeling Himalaya has seen several historical occurrences, each of which had a significant impact on the area. Additionally, the historic campaign for a separate state in the 1980s that shook West Bengal had a profound effect on the environment, ecology, and growth in the Queen of the Hills. There are several ways in which the agitation of the 1980s is connected to the significant environmental, social, economic, and political issues of the 1990s. Additionally, a thorough study of the region is necessary in light of current environmental issues in the Himalayan region.

III.4.   Profile of the Study Area:

(a)   Population:

Darjeeling district has 1,846,823 residents, which is almost equivalent to Kosovo's population, according to the 2011[28] census. As a result, it is ranked 257th out of 640 overall in India. 586 people live in the district for every square kilometre (1,520 for every square mile). Its population grew at a rate of 14.77% between 2001 and 2011.In Darjeeling, there are 970 girls for every 1000 men and 79.56% of people are literate. There were 1,595,181 people living in the Kalimpong district after it was divided, with 671,1771 (42.11%) of them residing in cities. The sex ratio in the residual district is 972 females for every 1000 males. The population is made up of 18.86% Scheduled Castes and 20.21% Scheduled Tribes, respectively.

In 2001, the population of the district was 1,609,172. There were 1,088,740 people living in rural areas and 520,432 people in urban areas. There were 778,528 women and 830,644 men overall. There were 511 people per square km. 23.79% was the annual population growth rate between 1991 and 2001.

There are 624,061 people living in the hills, or around 40% of the total population. The Lepchas or Rongpa (the ravine people, as they like to be called) were the first people to live in the Darjeeling Hills. The

---

28   *Census of India, 1991,2001 & 2011*

Limbu, Rai, Tamang, Gurung, Magar, Newar, Thami, Chettri, Bahun, Kami, and Damai are other long-established ethnic groups in the area. Since the 1950s, a sizable number of Tibetan immigrants from Tibet have also settled there. The boundaries between the hill people's and many ethnic groups have became fuzzier throughout time and today the majority identify as Gorkhas and speak Nepali exclusively as their mother tongue.

The largest ethnic group in the plains is Bengali, although there are also significant populations of Gorkhas and Adivasis, the later of whom moved from Chotanagpur and Santhal Parganas as tea garden labourers during British control. Biharis, Marwaris and Punjabis are among the migrants from other areas who live in both the plains and the hills.

(b) Caste & Religion:

Hinduism is the major religion in both the hills and plains. Buddhism and Kirat Mudhum are almost entirely present in the hills. Christianity is primarily prevailed in the hills, although there are significant numbers of them are the tea tribes in the plains. Islamism is almost entirely found in the plains.

39.88% of the population at the time of the 2011 census spoke Nepali as their mother tongue, followed by 26.51% Bengali, 10.95% Hindi, 6.17% Rajbongshi, 5.38% Sadri, 2.52% Kurukh, 1.50% Bhojpuri, and 1.15% Santali. As 'Others' under Bengali, 1.04% of the population have listed their language. In the three hill sub- divisions of the Darjeeling district (including Kalimpong), roughly 26% of the population, according to the 1951 Census, spoke Nepali as their mother tongue .In the past, the highlands were also home to the languages like Rai, Limbu, Tamang, Magar, Gurung, and Newar.[29]

The only subdivisions where Nepali has been designated as a co-official language are Darjeeling and Kurseong. Bengali is the district's

---

29 *Ibid.*

official language. Although the majority of hill residents are not from Khas groups, Nepali is the most common language in the hill divisions of Chatakpur, Sittong, Lamahatta, Kurseong, and Takdah in the Darjeeling Himalayas. More than 90% of the population speaks it. Even though the majority only speak Nepali now, many hundred of the original hill dwellers are still fluent in their native tongues.

(c) Sanitation and Water Supply:

Due to its age and inability to meet the requirements of the current population, the water delivery system is not as reliable as it once was. Nowadays, the life of people depends on access to private water sources and natural springs. A serious water issue hits the area during the summer and winter months. The family members then load Jerry cans with water from specified water sources and transport it to the homes.

Water shortages inevitably result in serious sanitary issues as well. Residential areas without septic tanks are in unsanitary conditions and increase the spread of illness. Uncertainty surrounds the effectiveness of the sanitary infrastructure that only covers 30% of Darjeeling. The lack of a comprehensive sewage disposal system in Darjeeling, as far as the municipality is concerned, causes unchecked sanitary problems that the authority neglects to address.

The existing water supply infrastructure was designed for a population of 15,000 in the years 1910 to 1915. Subsequently, a number of water supply infrastructure including Khangkhola Station, Rambi water line, Singdhap Lake (capacity of 15 million gallons) and Bangla Khola, were made, but they were unable to keep up with the population's rapid growth, leading to a severe water shortage from December to May. Due to the massive unlawful tree- felling that has occurred over the past several years, the water level at the catchments has rapidly decreased, heightening the issue. The number of people living in Darjeeling Town at now is in the lakhs, and the burden on the water supply grows rapidly with the addition of the floating population.

Darjeeling's town suffers from subpar sanitary standards. Due to improper management of liquid and solid wastes, the area's lands are being severely polluted. Here, 22% of homes lack access to latrines. Residents in squatter settlements rely on public restrooms, which are inadequately constructed in comparison to demand. Only 109 public restrooms are available across the city, out of a total of around 27,135 facilities. An average of 30 to 50 families depend on public lavatory facilities, according to a field survey. Public restrooms frequently become blocked owing to a shortage of water and improper paper disposal, a typical occurrence that goes unchecked and results in unusable conditions and poor cleanliness. People avoid travelling too far to urinate during the monsoon and winter months, which forces them to use open areas and sewers as toilets.

(d) Homestay:

"A period during which a visitor lives with a local family" is how the term "homestay" is defined. The purpose of the homestay programme is to house visitors with a local family, so they may become acquainted with their way of life, culture, natural surroundings, etc. The main sources of tourism in any rural region are homestays, which not only offer lodging and amenities but also the chance to experience rural life. In the Darjeeling Himalaya, some businesspeople opened brand-new homestays, while others converted pre-existing residences into homestays. It is a visit to a home by a traveler, most often a foreign student who is being hosted by a local family. The chance to fully experience the local culture is one of the main advantages of staying in a homestay. Living with a local family will provide you the opportunity to become familiar with their habits, traditions, and way of life.

(e) Education:

Around 73.5% of people in rural India were literate. In rural regions, 65% of women and 81% of men are literate. The shortage of instructors in rural regions is one of the biggest issues with education. Several other hindrances are found in the education sector which pull back the development of education in the region.

* Poorly Remunerated Teachers
* Non Attendance of the students
* Busy in Government Duties by the teachers
* Lack of Transport
* Poor Infrastructure
* Government Apathy

The guiding light of civilization is education. Another fascinating facet to discover in Darjeeling is the region's educational past.

(f) Society:

Darjeeling Himalaya is a region that is multilingual, multicultural, and multiethnic. The civilization in the region is made up of several components with origins from numerous places. The area's social variety may be its most potent expression. The many racial stocks, socioeconomic rank, and ethnically distinct social groupings have at various times found a place for themselves by adapting to the various ecological niches made available by the local physiographic and climatic environment. The bulk of the current residents were brought to the area by waves of immigration, who brought their forefathers from the neighbouring regions over the Himalayas. Their scattering has led to the development of a social mosaic with diverse ethnic characteristics. Approximately, the population of Darjeeling district may be broken down into the following ethnic groups:

* Nepalese, a general word that encompasses over 15 different ethnic groups. Various castes and tribes, such as the Sherpa, who arrived in the region from Nepal in the late 19th and early 20th century fall under this category.
* Lepcha (they are the autochthonous tribes in the area)
* Bhutia (A tribal group that comprises both Sikkimese and Bhutanese Bhutia)

- ❖   Tibetan (refugees that came to the area after 1961)
- ❖   Bengali (includes both permanent residents and migrants of south Bengal and refugees from Bangladesh)
- ❖   Other Indians

Political and economic conflicts have developed throughout time between the local indigenous population and foreigners. In this Himalayan region, frequent ethnic conflicts can take a serious turn. Additionally, there is a persistent push for Gorkha Land to become a distinct state. Most of the residents of the area, who are Nepalese, desire to form their own independent state outside of West Bengal.

III.4.   Economic Development and Sustainability of Rural Tourism:

Since many visitors today want to visit tranquil, lovely, nature- friendly, appealing, practical, clean, and pollution-free locations, rural tourism is a frequent trend. Rural tourism is becoming more important since it creates new businesses and job possibilities. It results in a blending of cultures and ethnicities. Additionally, it has a major impact on rural economies as well as the entire tourist sector. Sustainable development is the consequence of wise management of rural tourism in various rural locations.

III.4.1.   Role of Rural Tourism in Economic Development:

Owners, stakeholders, and people benefit financially from tourism, which boosts the economy of rural areas. In the long run, this increases per capita and national income. Rural tourism provides funding for the construction of roads, buildings, appropriate sanitation, proper drainage, and other rural infrastructure. Locals have benefited from rural tourism by getting jobs, while stakeholders have gained access to a range of commercial options. Sustainable land-use techniques are made possible in rural regions by rising revenue.

In general, sustainable tourism helps a place flourish economically. It shows up as an increase in income and employment opportunities, the development of infrastructure, and better living circumstances (Joshi and Dhyani, 2009[30]). The large influx of tourists and the ensuing economic activity at all of Darjeeling's local tourist attractions have sped up infrastructure construction while also creating employment and cash.

By providing opportunities for commerce and employment, as well as financial support, handicraft production, and historical preservation, rural tourism benefits indigenous people. It exposes people to a range of employment, livelihood, intercultural, and investment alternatives, enabling them to get a more comprehensive understanding of life. Along with the above mentioned benefits, it also helps to build cultural, socioeconomic, and cognitive abilities. In many rural places, the long-term survival of rural tourism depends on both environmental conservation and economic development. Local communities should be aware of the negative effects of the environment and act to preserve it in order to maintain its sustainability as the concept of sustainability gains popularity (Richards and Hall, 2000[31]).

Development of rural tourism benefits the community by fostering regional economic expansion. A field research at six rural tourism destinations was carried out to confirm the facts and theories that follow. Ten owners from each rural tourism destination were spoken to, and their incomes show how homestays have helped the local economies expansion. On the other hand, income growth fluctuates. Between 2013 and 2017, political movements and the occurrence of strikes that forced homestays to close for months and again during first quarter of 2020 to 2021 world wide Covid 19 pandemic led to a substantial fall in income.

---

30   *Joshi,R. & Dhyani, P.P (2009) ; 'Environmental Sustainability and Tourism – Implications of Trend Synergies of Tourism in Sikkim Himalaya' Current Science, Vol. 97, No. 1*

31   *Richards, G. & Hall,D (edt) (2000); 'Tourism and Sustainable Community Development', Routledge, London*

Chapter - IV

Data Analysis and Interpretation

This chapter explains the data analysis and discussions thereafter . Home-stay owners, businessman, students and drivers consulted in four Darjeeling Himalayan rural tourism destinations, namely Takdah, Lamahatta, Chatakpur, and Sittong, to obtain the necessary information. The quality of life can be described as an individual satisfaction with their living aspects in contrast to their desired existence. An individual's values and norms determine how an individual perceives his quality of life. The quality of working life is described as an integration of workplace strategies, techniques, and environment that promotes employees' job satisfaction.

IV.1. Occupation of the Respondents:

Sl No	Occupation of the Respondents	Percentage
1.	Business	85
2.	Student	4
3.	Driver	3
4.	Farmers	8

Table No. 4.1. Depicting the Occupation of the Respondents

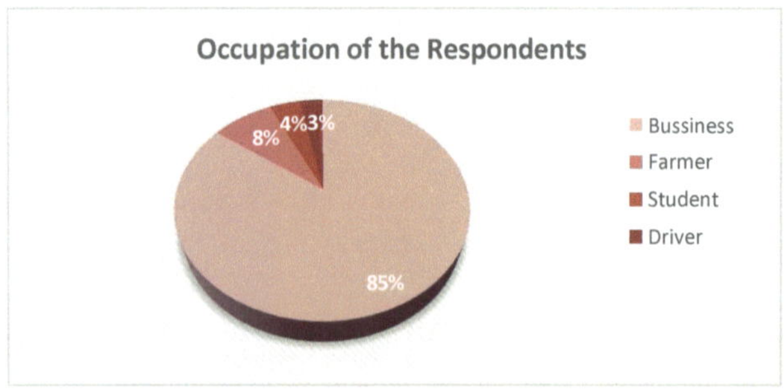

Occupation is a job or profession done by the people for their living. Accordingly to the data occupation was the keen topic of the people of Darjeeling Himalayas. These are the people with different occupations for the living and for earning for the family. It was founded that respondents had four main occupations namely businessman, farmer, student and driver. Businessmen (85%) were included mainly in the shops where fast foods & stationery goods are available and homestays also fall under the business category. The farmers (8%) involved mainly in the tea plantation in their own land and mostly few vegetable for their own use. It was also seen people produced their own tea by home procedure and serve the tourists the homemade tea. Next it was found that the students (4%) were also present who study and also help their parents with the business besides studying. Lastly there were a lot of drivers (3%) as they had their private vehicles who use their vehicles for tourists and also as an earning for their livelihood.

IV.2. Age Distribution of the Respondents:

Sl No.	Age (in years) of the Respondents	Percentage
1.	24 - 29	29
2.	29 - 34	20
3.	34 - 39	14
4.	39 - 44	13
5.	44 - 49	10
6.	49 - 54	9
7.	54 - 59	2
8.	59 - 64	1
9.	64 - 69	1
10.	69 - 74	1

Table No. 4.2. Depicting the Distribution of Age of the Respondents

The data in the above table shows the distribution of age of the respondents. It is found that respondents are in 24-29 years (29%), 29-

34 years (20%), 34-39 years (14%) , 39-44 years (13%), 44-49 years (10%), 49-54 years (9%), 54-59 years (2%) and 1% each in 59-64years, 64-69 years and 69-74 years.

Aged people do not try for resting at home instead working from morning to evening in the different farming areas they own. Females of the hills are mostly engaged in household chores or keep themselves busy in entertaining and working for the tourists those are visiting their homestays. Children go to school in the morning and by afternoon come home and help their mothers or fathers who are working in the fields. Age is not a key factor to them, whether old or young they are never tired of their work.

IV.3. Educational Qualification:

Sl. No.	Educational Qualification of the Respondents	Percentage
1.	P.G	3
2.	Graduate	18
3.	H.S. Pass	16
4.	High School Pass	46
5.	Under Matric	17

Table No. 4.3. Educational Qualification of the Respondents

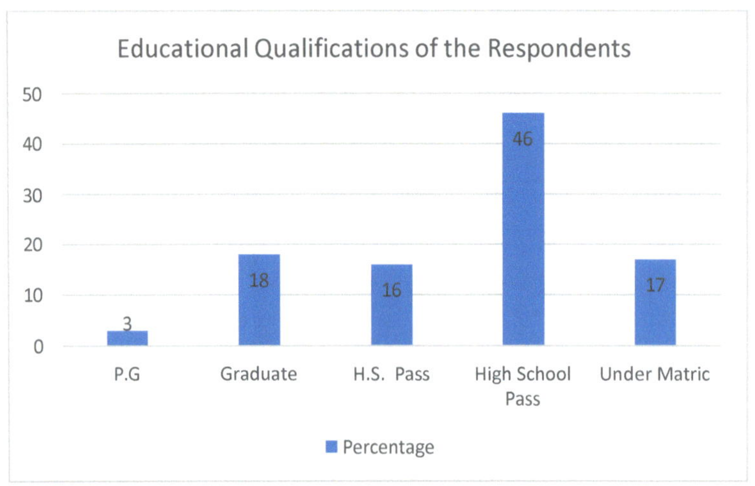

Education is one of the most important aspect of anyone's life. In today's world one needs to be educated and according to them the people of the rural areas are not highly educated. Opportunities are less granted and due to the distance, the educational opportunities of these areas are affected more in this area for their poor condition of infrastructure and poverty, though through rural tourism they are earning enough.

The study has been made in the rural areas of Darjeeling Himalayas-Chatakpur, Takdah, Lamahatta and Sittong, where it was found that the educational system is well developed even being rural areas. But more development would be more helpful as many areas don't have colleges yet. The schools and colleges both have played a great role in the development of the education system in these areas. The education system in these areas has improved a lot, not only by the efforts of the teachers but also by providing facilities of both indoor & outdoor sports & games.

Regarding educational qualifications of the respondents, 46 % were Matric pass, 18% were graduates, 17% were under matric, 16% were H.S Pass while 3% were having post-graduate qualifications. It is evident from the above data that none of the respondents were illiterate

IV.4. Religion:

Sl. No.	Religious Composition of the Study Area	Percentage
1.	Buddhist	75
2.	Christian	3
3.	Hindu	22

Table No. 4.4. Religious Composition of the Study Area

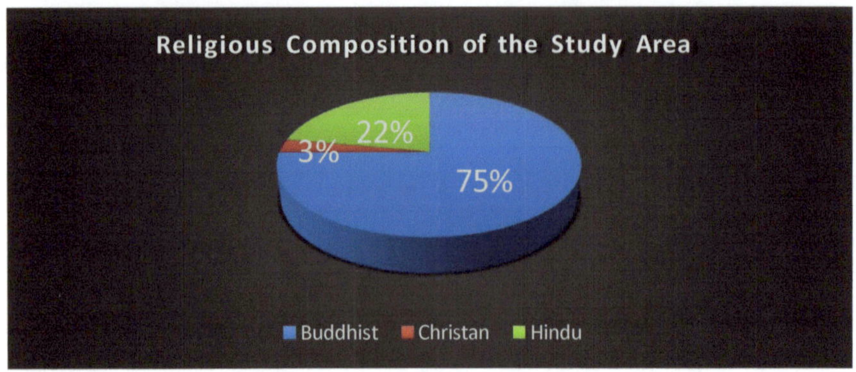

As it can be seen that in Darjeeling Himalayas there are many religions or caste but the areas of the Darjeeling Himalayas that were surveyed had mostly three religions in common, they were Buddhist, Christian and Hindu. Making a brief study and according to the pie chart it was found that the religion of the people of the areas of Sittong, Chatakpur, Takdah and Lamahatta that 75% population of the hills were Buddhist, 22% of them were Hindu and 2% of them follow Christianity.

IV.5. Best Months to Visit:

Sl No.	Places	Best Months to Visit
1.	Sittong	(Dec - May)
2.	Lamahatta	(Dec - May)
3.	Takdah	(Dec - May)
4.	Chattakpur	(Dec - May)

Table No. 4.5. Best Period to visit the Study Area.

The Hills have basically two peak tourist seasons those are from September to November and April to May. Tourist here mainly visit during the winters, that is from November to April or May. Evaluation has been made according to the peak time of visit in the four areas of the Darjeeling Himalayas in the diagram above. The temperature is ideal for a host of activities, whereas the summers can get uncomfortable for the tourist. So, the tourists prefer winter and spring season to visit the areas of the Darjeeling Himalayas.

IV.6. Preferences of Tourists:

Sl. No.	Places	Preferences of Tourist	
		Day Trip	**Night Trip**
1.	Sittong	18	4
2.	Takdah	25	0
3.	Chattakpur	13	15
4.	Lamahatta	24	1

Table No. 4.6. Preferences of Tourists to Visit the Study Area

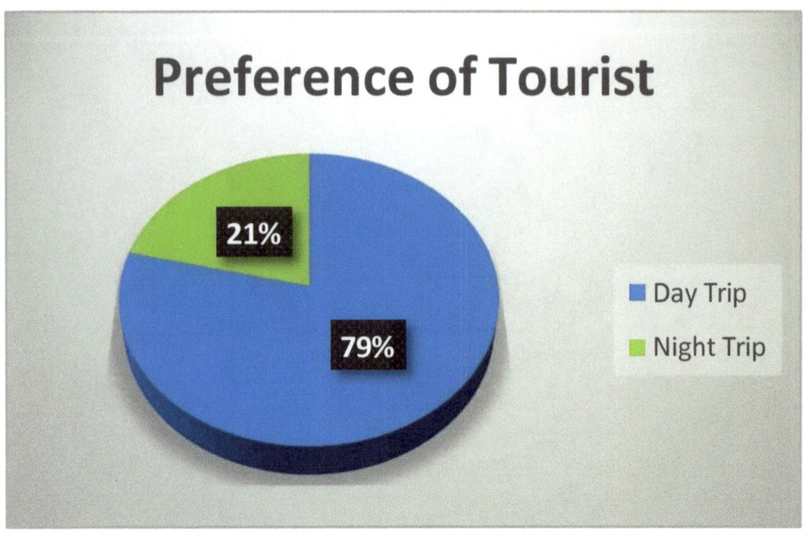

Data in the above depict the tourists' preference for either Day trip or a night trip at the study area and it have been collected from the entrepreneurs / owners of the homestays / businessmen. Visitors having different preferences according to the respondents found that the time of the visit for different tourists is either a day trip or a night trip. 79% of the tourists prefer day trip and the rest 21% of the people prefer night trip. It may vary from person to person. The tourists who visit here are mostly of the people of other states so they prefer day trips and the people of nearby towns and cities mostly come overnight for the stay. Though there is no problem for the respondents as they welcome the tourists with a warm heart and they can handle each tourist with care and guide them with huge care and hospitality.

IV.7.   Level of Satisfaction:

Facilities	Very Satisfactory	Satisfactory	Neutral	Un-Satisfactory	Very un-Satisfactory
Accommodation	65	25	10	0	0
Food Services	74	20	06	0	0
Attraction	80	20	00	0	0
Retail	45	35	12	08	0

Facilities	Very Satisfactory	Satisfactory	Neutral	Un-Satisfactory	Very un-Satisfactory
Information/ Visitors Centre	25	35	30	10	0
Way Finding Signage	30	28	32	10	0
Availability of Public Washrooms	25	30	35	10	0
Condition & Cleanliness of Public Toilets	35	25	25	15	0

Table No. 4.7. Level of Satisfaction of the Tourists to Visit the Study Area

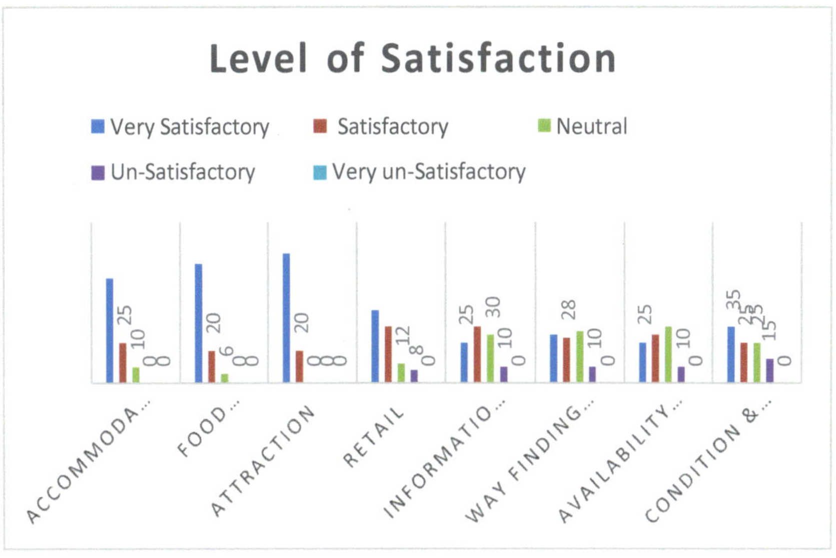

Data in the above show that the majority of the tourists are very much satisfied with the accommodation provided at the homestays (65 %); availability of food services by the homestays (74%) and attraction of the places of visit (80%); while tourists are satisfied with the retail outlet available at the tourist places but not satisfied with the information availability for the tourists, availability of public washroom and cleanliness of this public toilets, which need improvement.

IV.8. Facilities Required for Promotion of Rural Tourism:

Facilities	Indifferently	Low priority	Medium Priority	High Priority
Internet	0	0	0	100
Public Washroom	0	0	0	100
Local Transport	0	0	0	100
Roads	0	0	15	85
Promotion/ Marketing Support	0	10	20	70
Information/Visitor centre	0	0	20	80

Table No. 4.8. Facilities Required for Promotion of Rural Tourism

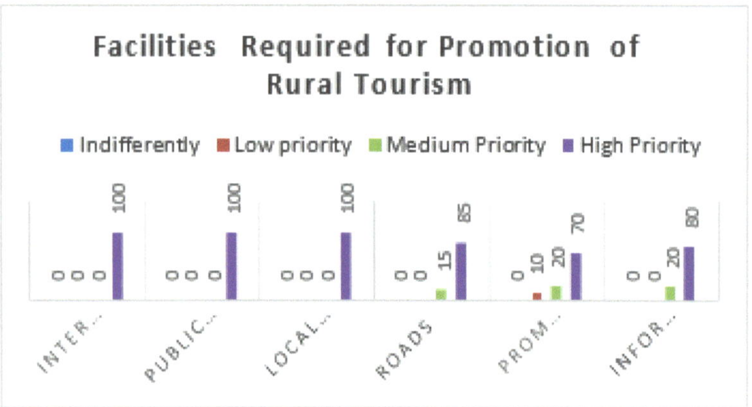

Data in the above explain about the opinion of different stakeholders regarding various facilities required for promotion of rural tourism in these tourist places. While all the stakeholders (100%) have opined that the development of internet facilities for communication, public washrooms, and local transport; 85% of the respondents have said that development of transport facilities; 70% were for the development promotion / marketing strategies and 80% have said that information should be widely circulated for the tourists about the places.

IV.9. Major Challenges to Rural Tourism:

Nature of Challenges	Strongly Agree	Agree	Neutral	Disagree	Strongly Disagree
Red Tape	35	52	13	0	0
Seasonal	85	15	0	0	0
Climate	70	25	5	0	0
Staffing	25	50	5	20	0
Housing	45	35	15	5	0
Internet/ Broadband	100	0	0	0	0
Promotion	70	20	10	0	0

Table No. 4.9. Major Challenges to Rural Tourism

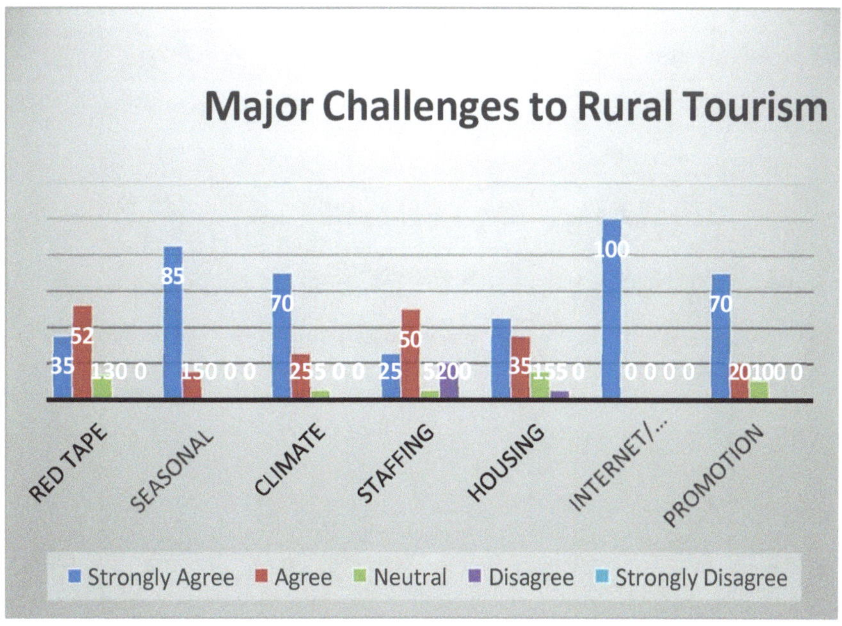

Data in the above illustrate about the opinion of different stakeholders regarding various challenges faced by them for promotion of rural tourism. While all the stakeholders (100%) have strongly agreed that development in the internet facilities for communication is the biggest challenge, sessional nature of the place (85%) and adverse climatic condition (70%) are the second and third biggest challenges. At the same time retaining permanent staff is a challenge for 50% of the stakeholders, development of the housing facilities due to shortage of land is strongly agreed by 45 % of the stakeholders and 52% of the respondents were strongly agreed that red-tapism is also challenge for them.

IV.10.   Rural Tourism and Economic Development:

Rural Tourism & Economic Development	Strongly Agree	Agree	Neutral	Disagree	Strongly Disagree
For the Individual	100	0	0	0	0
For the Locality	100	0	0	0	0
For the State	100	0	0	0	0
For the Nation	100	0	0	0	0

Table No. 4.10. Rural Tourism and Economic Development

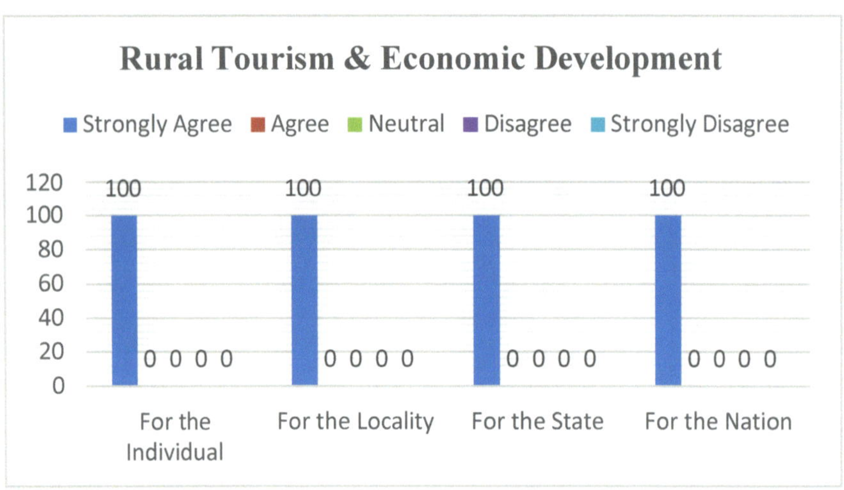

Regarding the contribution of rural tourism for the economic development, all the stake holders (100%) are strongly agreed to the fact that rural tourism helps for the economic development of the individual (Homestay owners / business men directly or indirectly associated with rural tourism), for the locality, for the state and the nation as a whole.

The city life is completely a different life from the rural areas of the Darjeeling Himalayas and one of the main reasons for their under development. If the roads and internet are put into consideration and looked into the matter seriously then the tourism of these areas would improve more. People will gain knowledge about the areas more and tend to visit more. More visits are equivalent to more income for them. However, it is noticed that the peak time of the visit of the areas are from November to May mostly but if the road facilities are improved then the people can add monsoon season too in their holidays lists to visit. As all know, during the monsoon season the mountains of North Bengal are mesmerizing to another level. The beauty of the mountains is more during the monsoon season but due to bad road conditions the tourists drop the idea to visit the mountains during the monsoon season. During the monsoon season there are more numbers of landslides occur and this becomes life threatening and life risking for the tourists who plan to visit in the monsoon season. The tourists compel to drop the idea of visiting the region during the monsoon season and for internet facilities.

Chapter - V

Findings, Conclusion and Recommendations

This chapter discusses the findings and recommendations drawn after a thorough investigation of rural tourism for sustainable development in the Darjeeling Himalayas.

Rural tourism has the potential to promote sustainable development through fostering economic growth and tourism development. Additionally, it offers a financially sound option for maintaining natural resources and raising the standard of living for locals. Rural tourism thus ensures the long-term viability of rural communities. To operate effectively, a healthy balance must be maintained between the daily operations of home-stay owners, stakeholders, local communities, visitors and the environment. To be sustainable, rural tourism must be both financially and socially practical as well as environmentally sound.

During the research, the author had come across various approaches to studying tourism, concepts and definitions of tourism, different types of tourism, concepts and types of rural tourism, understanding of sustainable development, and reviews and studies of rural tourism in the world, with a focus on India, West Bengal, and the Darjeeling

Himalaya in particular. After examining the published articles, studies, and papers, it was discovered that rural tourism in India started in the 1980s but really took off in the 1990s and beyond. It was believed that rural tourism is widespread and has established itself in its own niche. Regarding rural tourism in India, it is well known that both domestic and foreign visitors frequently travel to Darjeeling Himalaya rural tourism destinations in India, particularly in the spring and autumn, in order to experience peace and natural beauty. It is well understtod that rural tourism is essential to the long-term success of any region.

V.1.   Major Findings:

On the basis of the foregoing discussions, the major findings of the study were summed up as follows:

a)   Exceptional Tourist Influx:

It was found that domestic tourist arrivals in the Darjeeling Himalaya's rural tourism destinations, primarily Takdah, Lamahatta, Mineral Spring, Lepchajagat, Chatakpur, and Sittong, has increased five times higher between 2008 and 2017, whereas foreign visitors arrivals are doubled during the same time frame. With the influx of more domestic and international visitors than any other hill stations in India, Darjeeling is the most popular hill station in the country. The number of tourists remains significantly higher than the available lodging during the prime season, which is in the autumn and spring. Due to an overabundance of visitors, Darjeeling 94 Himalaya has already experienced a heat wave, and as a result, tourists are moving from the city to the villages. In terms of popularity, all rural tourist locations have seen an increase.

b)   The Steady Growth of Foreign Tourists:

The major foreign nations, including the United States, United Kingdom, Germany, France, Denmark, Canada, Sweden and Australia continue to be the principal sources of foreign tourists to all of the Darjeeling Himalaya tourism sites. Countries like France and Germany, during 2008 to 2017, the number of visitors visited the study areas have increased steadily. For the citizens of these nations, visiting Darjeeling is the desire to see friends and family.

c) The Steady Growth of Domestic Tourists:

Due to their close cultural ties, all rural tourist attractions in the Darjeeling Himalayas draw domestic visitors from various regions of West Bengal, Delhi, Mumbai, Orissa, Uttar Pradesh, Gujarat, Madhya Pradesh, Rajasthan, Maharashtra and Bihar in particular and the whole country in general. These states consistently send forth tourists.

d) Employment Opportunities:

The construction of home-stays, guest houses, and cottages in Darjeeling's rural areas has given ample job opportunities for the locals. All of the rural tourist attractions in the Darjeeling Himalayas are receiving employment chances through the Darjeeling Tourism Board. The majority of the neighborhood has benefited from the employment prospects brought forth by such home-stays; the best example is M.K. Pradhan, proprietor of Darjeeling Blossom Home- stay in Takdah, who provided jobs to 25 households.

e) Livelihood Opportunities and Standard of Living:

The local community as well as home-stay owners have benefited from the good livelihood opportunities provided by rural tourism in all of the Darjeeling Himalaya's rural tourism destinations. The majority of people who live in rural tourism areas have had the chance to benefit from rural tourism as well as to raise their standard of living. Since the beginning of rural tourism in their areas, everyone from the guesthouse owners to the local population has seen a significant improvement in their quality of life.

f) Social Services and Infrastructure:

All of the rural tourism destinations' have produced good social services and built out a solid infrastructure for visitors. The majority of respondents think that rural tourism in the Darjeeling Himalayas has increased the development of social amenities and infrastructure.

g)   Active Participation of Local Communities' in Rural Tourism:

Most of the members of the local community take advantage of the chance and actively participate in various rural tourism activities throughout the entire Darjeeling Himalaya region those are under study. Rural tourism has thrived in all of the places - thanks to the local community's understanding and active cooperation with the home-stay owners and tourists. The vicinity of the villages and the visitors have a tight relationship, which has aided in the expansion of rural tourism in the Darjeeling Himalayas. The impact of rural tourism has been handled by the locals more effectively than by any other tourism-related stakeholders. Home-stay proprietors and other stakeholders play a significant role in environmental protection, regardless of where they were located in the communities. All the parties involved in Darjeeling Himalayas' rural tourism destinations—hosts, the local community, and various travel agencies—exhibited active interest towards environmental protection.

V.2.   Impacts of Rural Tourism in Darjeeling Himalayas:

a)   Socio-economic Impacts:

According to the report, rural tourism's revenue has aided local governments and communities in modernizing their physical infrastructure, which has strengthened the region's economy as a whole. The health of nearby communities and rural tourism have both improved. Families who previously had no reliable source of income now have the choice to support a better way of life through rural tourism, and those who previously had a respectable and sustainable source of income could see a considerable rise in their income. It has benefited the local community irrespective of the social makeup to give the activity that is adequate from the economic point of view and constant over time. It has been observed that women and young people are more involved in rural tourism activities in the four rural tourist destinations of the Darjeeling Himalaya, namely Takdah, Lamahatta, Chatakpur, and Sittong. They work as a cook, guide, driver, receptionist, gardener, and manager in the host family, earning good wages and improving living standards.

Rural tourism has promoted social connection between visitors and local communities, which has led to mutual appreciation, comprehension forbearance, awareness, learning, positive relationships, mutual respect, and empathy. This has a positive societal impact. All of the Darjeeling Himalaya's rural tourism spots have subsequently benefited the local population. Visitors from all around India and the world had the chance to learn about regional traditions and customs. Additionally, the Darjeeling Himalaya's ethnicity and extravagant natural habitat draw tourists to the region, enabling the preservation of local customs, artistic creations, and hard work that had faced the threat of gradual extinction.

b) Cultural Impacts:

Assuming that it can benefit individuals of all races, countries and ethnicity and enhance cultural interactions between visitors and host communities, tourism has a huge cultural impact. Although this form of communication may have positive effects, it also has the potential to cause social unrest. It has been observed that there have been major cultural exchanges between locals and visitors in terms of language, knowledge, culture, traditions, and customs. Even while rural tourism has a substantial cultural impact in the study region, few members of the host community believe that it might breed animosity between locals and tourists.

c) Environmental Impacts:

The ecology is significantly impacted by rural tourism. While uninformed host communities and locals may contribute to environmental deterioration, educated stakeholders, host communities, local communities, and visitors may take positive action to safeguard the environment and raise public awareness.

V.3. Major Challenges to Rural Tourism in Darjeeling Himalayas:

From the study it is found that the stakeholders associated with rural tourism in Darjeeling Himalayas have faced numerous challenges for the promotion and sustainability of rural tourism of this region. Among these the major challenges are network issues for communication, poor road and transport facilities and infrastructure development, random climatic change and to some extent the cleanliness and upgradation of the public toilets in these tourist destinations. Though tourists are highly satisfied with the accommodation and food services available at these destinations, still wide circulation of the information about different facilities available at different destinations are need to be improved for more influx of tourists and sustainability of the rural tourism.

V.4. Recommendations:

On the basis of the findings, the following recommendations are pertinent for the promotion and sustainability of rural tourism in Darjeeling Himalayas.

- ❖ To ensure that tourism does not negatively impact communities' governance structures, lives or biodiversity, policies, guidelines so that rules for rural tourism should be updated.
- ❖ The host community and the local community should receive financial aid from the government and private organizations, as well as the necessary training and developing capacity programmes, in order to develop their life skills, improve their communication skills, and manage tourism for different types of tourists effectively. Adequate training must also be ensured

for the host communities in order to offer excellent amenities to the tourists and consequently, for the successful operation of tourism industry.

- To keep rural tourism regions clean and hygienic, the government, host communities, neighbourhood residents, all parties involved, and business organizations should take action. All rural tourism locations should be established plastic-free zones since garbage disposal and proper management are important for improving rural tourism. All rural tourist places should utilize enough trash cans or naturally occurring bamboo trash cans, and they should separate their biodegradable and non-biodegradable waste. This will help to maintain the environment clean.

- Many public sector departments involved in the tourism industry must collaborate, coordinate their tasks, and keep one another informed of their activities and strategies.

- Anything made out of plastic such as holders, cups, containers or water jugs should be tallied upon entering the forest areas for untamed life observation or travel, and any slips should be severely disciplined.

- The administration of the tourism sector in Darjeeling Himalayas is required to hire at least a certain percentage of local residents as employees, in order to stimulate local investment.

- To lessen strain on the areas supporting natural life, many additional prospective rural tourism zones should be made accessible to visitors.

- Different types of pollution should be managed in all of Darjeeling Himalaya's rural areas. Anti-littering regulations need to be strengthened.

- All of Darjeeling Himalaya's rural tourism businesses should emphasis on market locally made goods to visitors.

- The serious consideration of the concerned experts is required due to the bad condition of the roads in numerous rural tourist locations in the Darjeeling Himalaya. All-weather highways should be built by the government to enhance transport and draw in tourists from abroad. The support job must be completed correctly and on schedule.

* An environmental tax could be collected from visitors at the entry gate in remote tourist locations, typically in forest settlements like Chatakpur, and Lamahatta for environmental protection & sustainability.

* The creation of various websites, periodicals, Facebook pages, and videos over different social media apps can be used to promote to further enhance/encourage the rural tourism in all of the rural Darjeeling Himalayan destinations.

* Broadly highlighting the anthropogenic and natural potentials of rural tourism in the Darjeeling Himalaya must be done via all media platforms.

V.5.   Scope for Further Research:

Today's society requires sustainable development in all areas and there is still scope to investigate this idea and its potential applications in the tourist sector, the service sector with the greatest rate of growth worldwide. More research is required to evaluate the sustainable rural tourism initiatives implemented by local governments in the Darjeeling Himalayas. Additionally, there is a huge opportunity for scholars to suggest a sustainable rural tourist strategy for other Darjeeling Himalayan places with a comparable Eco-system.

The dropout study opens the door for extensive tourism planning and development for the long-term advantages and overall development of the Darjeeling Himalayas. An Integrated Environmental Impact Assessment (EIA) based on a specific project should be carried out by a multidisciplinary team of experts to examine the potential benefits and dangers of the planned tourism project.

The opportunity for groundbreaking research lies in the discovery and advancement of untapped rural tourism spots in the Darjeeling Himalayas, offering unexplored and pristine experiences.

Bibliography

Aggarwal, P. (1999); 'Tourism and Economic Growth and Development', New Delhi, Mohit Publications.

Ahamed Mustak (2018); "Rural Tourism as a Sustainable Development Alternative: An Analysis With Special Reference To Ballavpur Danga Near Santiniketan, West Bengal (India)", IOSR Journal of Business and Management (IOSR-JBM)

Aneja, P. (2006); "Sustainable Tourism Development Challenges Ahead". Kurukshetra, Vol. 12, No. 5.

Aslam M.S.M., Khairil,A.W, Nor'ain.O.B (2014). "Issues and Challenges in Nurturing Sustainable Rural Tourism Development", Tourism, Leisure and Global Change, Volume 1 (2014).

Aytug, K. H., Mikaeili, M. (2016). "Evaluation of Hopa's Rural Tourism Potential in the Context of European Union Tourism Policy", Elsevier, Vol. 37, No. 1.

Badan, B. S., Bhatt, H. (2006); 'Sustainable Tourism', New Delhi, Kanishka Publishers and Distributors.

Bande, U. (2002); "Eco-Tourism and Mountains". Yojana, Vol. 24, No.15 (August).

Banerjee, S., (2001); "Darjeeling in Doldrums Again", www.bengalathenet.com

Bharath Bhushan, E. K. (2005). "Sustainable Tourism Development". Kerala Calling, Vol.50, No.16, (October).

Bhatia A. K., (1991). 'Tourism Development: Principles and Practices', New Delhi, Sterling Publishers Private Limited.

Bhattacharya, P. (2008). "Tourism Development in Northeast India: Changing Recreational Demand, Developmental Challenges and Issues associated with Sustainability", European Bulletin of Himalayan Research, Vol. 3, No. 1

Bhujel, R.B., (1993); "Darjeeling Hills: Its Environmental Status", Paper Unpublished.

Bhutia, Y. (1991); "Natural Environment and Changing Socio-economic setup in Darjeeling Himalaya", M.Phil Dissertation (unpublished) submitted to CSRD, JNU.

Biswas, S., (1987); "Rural Development in the Hill Areas: A study of two villages in Kalimpong", Occasional Paper-3, Darjeeling, CHS, North Bengal University.

Bojnec Stefan (2010). "Rural Tourism, Rural Economy Diversification, and Sustainable Development", Academica Turistica, Year 3, No. 1– 2, July.

Brundtland Report (1987); 'World Commission on Environment and Development'

Burja Camelia, Burja Vasile (2014); "Sustainable Development of Rural Areas: A Challenge for Romania", Environmental Engineering and Management Journal, Vol.13, No. 8, August 2014

Caprihan, K. V., Kirthi, S. (2004); "Eco-Tourism in India". South Asian Journal of Socio-Political Studies (SAJOSPS), Vol.12, No.2 (Jan-June).

Census of India, 1991,2001 & 2011; "District Census Hand Book", West Bengal, Darjeeling District.

Chakraborty, K. C. (1986); "The Tourists of Darjeeling: A Survey", The Eastern Himalayas: Environment and Economy (Ed.) in R. L. Sarkar and M.P.Lama, Eastern Himalayas: Environment and Economy, Institute of Hill Economy, Darjeeling, pp. 412-426.

Chakraborty, P.K., (1988); "Ecology and Environmental Planning in the Darjeeling Himalaya", in Chadha, S.K. edited 'Himalayas: Ecology and Environment', New Delhi, Mittal Publications. Pp.137 - 149.

Chakraborty, P.K., (1989); "Darjeeling Himalaya: A Study in Environmental Degradation", in Chadha, S.K. edited Ecological Hazards in the Himalayas, Jaipur, Painter Publisher. Pp. 133 - 143.

Chamy Anthony, (2001). "Accessible Sustainable Ecotourism: Necessary Market Adjustments in a New Age of Travel". ecotoursonline.ca.

Chand, M., Bhushan, R. (2005). "Rural Tourism: A New Approach to Sustainability". South Asian Journal of Socio-Political Studies (SAJOSPS), Vol.9, No.2 (Jan-June).

Chaturvedi Devesh, (2010). "Tourism in India: Ensuring Buoyancy and Sustainability". Yojana, Vol.13, No.8, May.

Chawla Ramesh (2006). 'Ecology and Tourism Development', First Edition, New Delhi, Sumit Enterprises.

Chettri, N. (1998). "Impact of Tourism on Biodiversity: A Case Study from the Sikkim Himalayas, India". South Asian Perspectives in Eco-tourism and Conservation, Gangtok: Ecotourism and Conservation Society of Sikkim.

Cronin, L. (1990); 'A Strategy for Tourism and Sustainable Developments', World Leisure and Recreation 32(3), pp. 12-18.

D' Souza Rohin (2009).'Rural Development Through Rural Tourism', Salesian Journal, New Delhi, Kalpa Griha Publication.

Das, Niranjan, H. J. Syiemlieh, (2004). "Eco-Tourism in Assam".Yojana, Vol.8, No.4 (July)

Dashper, K. (2014); 'Rural Tourism: An International Perspective', Cambridge Scholars Publishing, Newcastle, UK.

Development of Rural Tourism in the Region of Gruza, Serbia", Procedia Environmental Sciences, Vol. 14, No.1 (2011).

Diganta K., Mudoi R. (2011); "Tourism Sector in North East Region of India", Southern Economist, (2011) Vol. 50 (11), pp. 49-51.

Dimitrovski, D. D. (2011). "Rural Tourism and Regional Development: Case study of Development of Rural Tourism in the Region of Gruza, Serbia", Procedia Environmental Sciences, Vol. 14, No.1

Dodds, R. & Butler, R. (2010); 'Barriers to Implementing Sustainable Tourism Policy in Mass Tourism Destinations, Tourism';os, Volume 5, No.1, pp.35-54.

Dordevic, Z. D., Susic, V., Janjic, I. (2019); "Perspectives of Development of Rural Tourism of the Republic Of Serbia", Economic Themes, Vol.1 No.1.

Dorji P., Kinley (2017); "Rural Tourism in Bhutan: A Tool to Achieve Gross National Happiness", Journal of Hospitality Tourism, Vol. 4, No. 2, March.

Drgulanescu Irina Virginia, Drutu Maricica (2012); "Rural Tourism for Local Economic Development", International Journal of Academic Research in Accounting, Finance and Management Sciences, Volume 2, Special Issue 1 (2012), pp. 196-203

Drgulanescu Irina Virginia, Drutu Maricica (2012); "Rural Tourism for Local Economic Development", International Journal of Academic Research in Accounting, Finance and

Frederick, M. (1992); 'Tourism as a Rural Economic Development Tool: An Exploration of the Literature', U.S. Department of Agriculture, Economic Research Service.

Gale, T., Hill, J. (2009); 'Ecotourism and Environmental Sustainability Principles and Practice', Bristol (U.K.), Routledge Publication.

Gangotia, A. (2013); "Home Stay Scheme in Himachal Pradesh: A Successful Story of Community Based Tourism Initiatives (CBTIS)", Global Research Analysis, Vol.2, Issue 2.

Gartner, W.C (2004); 'Rural Tourism Development in USA'; International Journal of Tourism Research, Vol.6 (3), May-June, Bristol(U.K.), Gate Publication.

Geography and You, (2002): "Seeking Solutions for our Barren Slopes" Vol. 2, No. 1, Pp. 4 -13.

Gursoy D., Jurowski C., Uysal M. (2002); "Resident Attitudes: A Structural Modeling Approach". Annals of Tourism Research, Vol. 1 No.1.

Hall Michael and Alan Addison (1999);"Sustainable Tourism-A Geographical Perspective". International Journal of Tourism Research, Vol. 2, Issue 5.

Henderson, et al. (2001). "Urban Environmental and Nature-Based Attractions: Green Tourism in Singapore". Tourism Recreation Research, Vol. 26 (3).

Hill Jennifer and Timgale (2000);"Ecotourism and Environmental Sustainability Principles and Practice". Research

Hunziker W., Krapf K. (1942); "General Tourist Theory". The Outline of General Tourism Science, Vol. 26, No. 3.

Irshad, H. (2010); 'Rural Tourism - An Overview, Agriculture and Rural Development', Government of Alberta, Rural Development Division, October.

Jagmohan, N. (1990); 'Tourism and Travel', New Delhi, Gitanjali Publishing House.

N. Jayapalan, (1984). 'An Introduction to Tourism', Delhi, Atlantic Publishers and Distributors.

Joshi,R. & Dhyani, P.P (2009) ; 'Environmental Sustainability and Tourism – Implications of Trend Synergies of Tourism in Sikkim Himalayas' Current Science, Vol. 97, No. 1.

Joshi, S.C., (1984); "Rural Development in the Himalaya - Problems and Prospects", Nainital, Gyanodaya Prakashan,

Kandari and Ashish Chandra (2003); "Tourism, Bio-diversity Sustainable Development". New Delhi, Isha Books Publication, , Vol. 4, Issue 3.

Katoch, A., Prashant, G. (2015); "Rural Tourism as a Medium for Local Development in Himachal Pradesh: The example of Villages around Dharamshala (Kangra)". South Asian Journal for Tourism and Heritage, Vol. 8, No.1.

Kazana, V., Kazaklis, A. Merou, Th., Takos, I. (2009); 'Fuzzy Multi-Criteria Modelling for Impact Assessment in the Context of Sustainable Forest Management. A Greek Case Study'. In: M. Palahi, Y. Birot, F. Bravo and E. Gorriz (eds), EFI Proceedings 57, pp 175-184

Khawas, V., (2001); "Untold Story of Gorkhaland Agitation", Paper Unpublished.

Kiper, T. (2013); "Role of Ecotourism in Sustainable Tourism", Advances in Landscape Architecture, Intech, Vol. 1, No. 1.

Kohli, M. S. (2002); "Eco-Tourism and Himalayas". Yojana, Vol.24, No.15 (August).

Kumar, S., Sampad, M. (2007); "Eco-Tourism and Sustainable Development-A Case Study of Chandaka Wildlife Sanctuary in

Orissa". South Asian Journal of Socio-Political Studies (SAJOSPS), Vol.7, No.2.

Lane, B. (2009); "Rural Tourism: An Overview", The SAGE Handbook of Tourism Studies, (Ed. Tazim Jamal and Mike Robinson), SAGE Publications, Vol.1, No. 1.

Lane, B. (2009); "What is Rural Tourism", Journal of Sustainable Tourism, Vol. 2, Issue 1 (August 2009)

Lepp, A. (2007); "Residents' Attitudes Towards Tourism in Bigodi Village, Uganda". Elselvier, March (2007) Volume 8, No.8.

Liu, J. C., Sheldon, P. J. and T. Var, (1987); "Resident Perceptions of the Environmental Impacts of Tourism", Annals of Tourism Research.

Liu, Z. (2003); "Sustainable Tourism Development: A Critique", Journal of Sustainable Tourism, Vol. 11, No. 6

Malek Abdul, Anand H., (1993); "Economic and Environmental Impacts of Tourism in Socotra Island", Southern Economist, Vol.48, No.4.

Manoj, K. P. (2016); "Impact of Rural Tourism on the Environment and Society: Evidence from Kumbalangi in Kerala, India", International Journal of Advanced Research in Computer Science and Management, Vol. 4, No. 2 (February 2016).

Martin S. R., and S.F. McCool, (1992); "Attitude of Montana Residents towards Tourism Development" .Research Report 23. Missoula.

MT: The University of Montana, School of Forestry, Institute for Tourism and Recreation Research 21.

McIntosh, W. R., Goeldner, R. C. (1986); 'Tourism: Principles, Practices', Philosophies, Wiley Publisher.

Mili Nitashree, (2012); "Rural Tourism Development: An Overview of Tourism in the Tipam Phakey Village of Naharkhatia in Dibrugarh District, Assam, India". International Journal of Scientific and Research Publications, Vol. 2.Issue 12.

Mohanlal,K.G. (2007); "Eco-tourism in Kerala". South Asian Journal of Socio-Political Studies (SAJOSPS), Vol.18, No.1 (July-Dec 2007).

Mousavi, S. S., Doratli, N., Mousavi, S.N., Moradiahari, F. (2016); "Defining Cultural Tourism", International Conference on Civil, Architecture and Sustainable Development, Vol. 1, No. 1, (December).

Mrksa Milutin, Gajic Tamara (2014); "Opportunities for Sustainable Development of Rural Tourism in The Municipality Of VRBAS", Economics of Agriculture 1/2014, UDC: 338-44(1-22)

Murti, S.K & Kumar S. (1989); 'Tourists Activities Causing Depletion of Plant Wealth in Jammu & Kashmir, In Impacts of Tourism on Mountain Environment', (ed. S.C. Singh) Research India Publications.

Nomani, A., Khan, R.K.M. (2015); "Human Resource Development in Tourism Industry – An Analytical Framework", South

Asian Journal for Tourism and Heritage (SAJTH), Vol. 8. No. 1.

Nooripoor, et al. (2020); "The Role of Tourism in Rural Development: Evidence from Iran", Geo Journal, Vol.1, No.1.

O'Malley, L. S. S. (1907); 'Bengal District Gazetteer: Darjeeling'.

Calcutta: The Bengal Secretariat Book Depot.

Okech, et al. (2012). "Rural Tourism as a Sustainable Development Alternative: An Analysis with Special Reference to Luanda, Kenya", Culture, Vol. 3, No.1. (August).

O'malley, L.S.S., (1907); "Darjeeling District Gazetteers, Calcutta.

Panda, T. K., Mishra, S., Parida, B. B. (1992); 'Tourism Management: The Socio-Economic and Ecological Perspective' Hyderabad: Universities Press.

Pandya, M.T., Oza, G. M. (1994); "Biodiversity for the Masses". Indian Forester, Vol. 20, No1.

Pearce, J. (1980); "Host Community Acceptance of Foreign Tourists: Strategic Considerations", Annals of Tourism Research, Vol. 7, Issue 2.

Perez, E. A., Nadal, J. R. (2005); "Host Community Perceptions: A Cluster Analysis". Annals of Tourism Research, Vol. 32, No. 4.

Pizam, A., Milman, A. (1986); "The Social Impacts of Tourism", Tourism Recreation Research, Vol. 11, No. 1

Rajan, J., Sabu, K. T., (2001); "Impact of Tourism on the Environment of Munnar". Review of Social Sciences, Vol. 1, No. 1.

Rao, K.S. & Saxena, K. G., (1994); "Sustainable Development and Rehabilitation of the Degraded Village Lands in Himalaya", Dehra Dun,Bishen Singh Mahendra Pal Singh.

Reid,D. (1995); 'Sustainable Development: An Introductory Guide', London, Routledge.

Repetto, R. (1985); 'The Global Possible: Resources, Development, and the New Century', (World Resources Institute Book), New Haven and London, Yale University Press.

Richards, G. & Hall,D (edt) (2000); 'Tourism and Sustainable Community Development', London, Routledge,

Richardson, J. I. and Fluker, M. (2004); 'Understanding and Managing Tourism'. Frenchs Forest, NSW: Pearson Education Australia.

Roy, B., (1968): "Darjeeling District Census Handbook- 1961", Calcutta.

Sethi, P. (2002); 'Millennium Trends in Travel and Tourism', Delhi, Rajat Publications.

Sharma, V. (1985); "Tourism: It's Socio-Economic Importance". Southern Economist, Vol. 24, No.14.

Sharpley, R. (2000); Tourism and sustainable development: exploring the theoretical divide, Journal of Sustainable Tourism 8(1), pp. 1-19.

Singh, S. (1997); 'Eco-tourism and Environmental Conservation in India', New Delhi, Rajat Publication.

Singh, T.V. & Kaur, J. (Eds.), (1985); "Integrated Mountain Development", New Delhi, Himalayan Books .

Spychala, A., Sylwia G. (2013); "What is Nature Tourism? Case Study of University Students". Turyzm, Vol. 1, No.1.

Stettner, A. C. (1993). "Community or Commodity? Sustainable Development in Mountain Resorts". Tourism Recreation Research, Vol. 18, No. 1.

Stojanovic, M., Stojanovic, D., Randelovic, D. (2010); "New Trends in Participation at Tourist Market under Conditions of Global Economic Crisis", Tourism and Hospitality Management, Vo. 1, No. 1.

Sunlu, U. (2003); "Environmental Impacts of Tourism", CIHEAM, Vol. 1, No. 1

Timilsina P (2012); "Homestay Tourism Boosts Ghale Gaon's Economy". Retrieved from http://www.gorkhapatra. org.np./ rising.detail. php?Article_id=23200&cat_id=4. On 10 June 2024.

Timilsina, P. (2012); "Home-stay Tourism Boosts Ghale Gaon's Economy", Gorkhapatra, Vol.1, No.1.

Tosun, C., Timothy, J. D. (2003); "Arguments for Community Participation in the Tourism Development Process", The Journal of Tourism Studies, Vol. 14, No. 2.

Upadhyay, P. (2016); "Envisaged for Sustainable Rural Development: Viability and Challenges of Rural Tourism in Nepal", Repositioning, Vol. 1, No. 1.

Var, T., Sheldon, P. J. and Liu, J. C. (1987); "Resident Perceptions of the Environmental Impacts of Tourism". Annals of Tourism Research.

Ziffer, A. K. (1989); 'Ecotourism: The Uneasy Alliance', Conservation International, Ernst and Young, Washington D.C.

Questionnaire for Entrepreneurs

A. PERSONAL INFORMATION:

1. Name-
2. Area-
3. Age-
4. Sex-
5. Level of Education-
6. Occupation-
7. Municipality-
8. Are you employed? (Yes/No)-
9. Position in the household-
10. Religion-
11. Marital Status-
12. Family pattern- Nuclear/Joint/Extended

B. ENTERPRISE:

13. Land or Area owned:
14. Where are all the main activities carried out in the farm?
15. How many employees are working under you?

C. RURAL TOURISM PRODUCT DEVELOPMENT:

16. What do you think about tourism in this site?
17. Do you think the tourism can help to increase your income or it can generate more employment opportunities?
18. Would you put suggestions to attract more tourists to the village?
19. What do you feel about activities of the local government for the improvement of the area?

20. Would you like to involve/invest in tourism activities? If no, why?

21. Do you feel a training need for income generation?

D. COMMUNICATION:

22. What are the main modes of communication in the locality?

23. Do they have any banking facilities?
    - If yes, what kind of services are offered like savings?
    - How many involved in banking Service?

E. TOURISM DEVELOPMENT:

24. How do they spent their leisure time?

25. Questions of traditional food / cultural activities / festivals / sports / handicrafts / old customs / monastery ?

26. Have you ever been as a tourist?

27. If you get any external funds, are you interested to involve in the business?

28. Total number of schools / colleges?

29. Any hospitals / nursing home?

30. Any extra requirement from Government for improvement in Infrastructure?

31. To whom you approach to get advice for a new initiatives?

32. Does tourism have impact on local people and in what ways?

33. How many home stays you own?

34. What are the main attribution of Rural Tourism here?

35. Any guides available in the village?

36. When was the home stay built?

37. Number of the tourists visited in your home stay till date?

38. What is the best season to visit this place?

39. How was your life before home stay and after home stay ?

40. Are the land on lease or own?-

41. Any improvement in new employment in new due to tourists?

42. How would you the rate the following as assets, infrastructures you would like to see developed to support tourism?

Facilities	Indifferently	Low priority	Medium Priority	High Priority
Internet				
Public Washroom				
Local Transport				
Roads				
Promotion/ Marketing Support				
Information/ Visitor centre				

43. Please estimate the percentage of your visitors that comes for a day trip and the percentage that are overnight visitors?

Day Trip -   Night Trip -

44. On average, how many nights does a typical visitor stay?

45. Are visitors to this business most likely to be?

Families ☐   solo ☐   Couples ☐   Seniors ☐   Business ☐ Groups ☐

46. How would you rate the following challenges to operating a tourism business in this area?

Nature of Challenges	Strongly Agree	Agree	Neutral	Disagree	Strongly Disagree
Red Tape					
Seasonal					
Climate					
Staffing					
Housing					
Internet/ Broadband					
Promotion					

47. Rate your level of satisfaction on the tourism facilities availability in this area:-

Facilities	Very Satisfactory	Satisfactory	Neutral	Un-Satisfactory	Very un-Satisfactory
Accommodation					
Food Services					
Attraction					
Retail					
Information/ Visitors Centre					
Way finding Signage					
Availability of Public Washrooms					
Condition & Cleanliness of public toilets					

F. TOURISM SURVEY:-

49. How does local markets gets affected in this business?

50. Are you involved with the following organization:

    a) Regional Tourism organization   Yes/ No/ I Don't Know

    b) Destination Management Marketing Organization Yes/No/I Don't Know

51. If yes to DMO, please specify the organization?

52. Are you a member of other tourism organization? If yes, Specify?

53. Do you offer packages?

54. What methods do you use to promote your business?

55. Any improvement in new employment due to tourists?

56. Any new business started due to tourism ?

Questionnaire for Tourists

A. PERSONAL INFORMATION:
1. Name -
2. Area -
3. Age -
4. Sex -
5. Level of Education -
6. Occupation -
7. Municipality -
8. Are you employed? (Yes/No) -
9. Position in the household -
10. Religion -
11. Marital Status -
12. Family pattern - Nuclear/Joint/Extended

B. RURAL TOURISM PRODUCT DEVELOPMENT:
13. What do you think about tourism in this site?
14. What do you feel about activities of the local government for the improvement of the area?

B. TOURISM DEVELOPMENT:
15. How do they spent your leisure time?
16. Have you ever been as a tourist?
17. Do you prepare any annual plan for touring different places during your leisure time? Yes / No
    a) If yes, do you keep special budget for this?
18. What are the main attribution of Rural Tourism here?
19. Any guides available in the village?

20. How would you the rate the following as assets, infrastructures you would like to see developed to support tourism?

Facilities	Indifferently	Low priority	Medium Priority	High Priority
Internet				
Public Washroom				
Local Transport				
Roads				
Promotion/ Marketing Support				
Information/Visitor centre				

21. How would you rate the following challenges to operating a tourism business in this area?

Nature of Challenges	Strongly Agree	Agree	Neutral	Disagree	Strongly Disagree
Red Tape					
Seasonal					
Climate					
Staffing					
Housing					
Internet/ Broadband					
Promotion					

22.   Rate your level of satisfaction on the tourism facilities availability in this area:

Facilities	Very Satisfactory	Satisfactory	Neutral	Un-Satisfactory	Very un-Satisfactory
Accommodation					
Food Services					
Attraction					
Retail					
Information/ Visitors Centre					
Way finding Signage					
Availability of Public Washrooms					
Condition & Cleanliness of public toilets					

23.   Please tell the reason(s) for visiting this site:

Reasons	Strongly Agree	Agree	Neutral	Disagree	Strongly Disagree
Attraction					
Accommodation					
Accessibility					
Amenities					
Awareness					

www.ingramcontent.com/pod-product-compliance
Lightning Source LLC
Chambersburg PA
CBHW040910110726
48005CB00006B/863